PULSE
REVOLUTION

Tami Hardeman

CONTENTS

INTRODUCTION
TO PULSES

WHAT ARE PULSES?

From the Latin word *puls*, meaning porridge or thick soup, pulses are the dried, edible seeds of a legume plant. Nutritious and sustainable, they are an integral part of many cuisines and an easy way to put protein on your plate.

A KITCHEN STAPLE

Tasty and versatile, pulses are a class of legume. Unlike other legume pods that are fresh-harvested or fatty (such as fresh beans, fresh peas, peanuts, and soybeans), pulses are harvested after they've dried within the pod. The dehydrated seeds are an inexpensive protein source that you can store for years, making them a pantry staple. Once cooked, pulses can be enjoyed in a host of applications, from sweet to savory. Whether they are braised, roasted, sprouted, or puréed, pulses are embraced by vegetarians, vegans, and omnivores alike for their nutrition, convenience, and flavor.

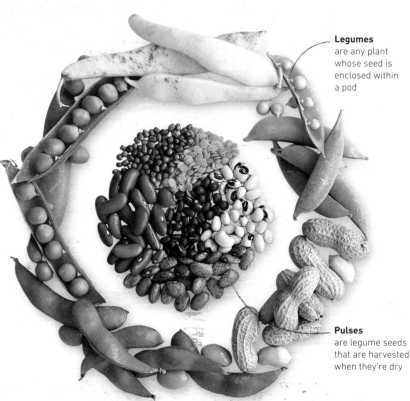

Legumes
are any plant whose seed is enclosed within a pod

Pulses
are legume seeds that are harvested when they're dry

HOW THEY'RE GROWN AND HARVESTED

Unlike many legumes, pulses are dry-harvested once fully mature. Home cooks then re-hydrate the seeds by soaking in liquid so they're suitable for cooking.

1
Farmers choose and plant their seeds during spring in the northern hemisphere and late fall in the southern hemisphere. Wet weather is best for planting.

2
Farmers may roll crop beds flat after planting to improve harvest rates. Low-hanging pods are less likely to break when they're cleanly separated from the soil.

3
The pods mature through the next season. Dry weather is ideal for harvesting, so some farmers apply chemicals to aid drying, especially during cold, wet seasons.

ALL SHAPES & SIZES

From tiny beluga lentils to giant fava beans, pulses come in a vast array of sizes, colors, and textures. They are often grouped into four categories—dry beans, dry peas, lentils, and chickpeas—all of which are easy to prepare and packed with fiber and protein.

DRY BEANS

The varieties of dry beans are virtually boundless, but each type is nutritionally dense and deliciously versatile. Cook your beans in batches, then experiment with their unique flavors and textures by incorporating them into a variety of different dishes.

DRY PEAS

Unlike fresh peas, which are often eaten directly from the pod, dry peas are harvested and shelled once fully mature. Available both split and whole, these pulses have a slightly sweet, earthy flavor and a thick, creamy texture that makes them ideal for soups.

LENTILS

Available in a range of colors and sizes, these tiny lens-shaped seeds are sold both split and whole. They don't require soaking, so they're quick to cook and hold their shape well. The flavor and texture of lentils are especially suited to soups, salads, and braises.

CHICKPEAS

Also called garbanzo beans, this pulse variety has a distinct hazelnut-like shape. Often found in Indian and Mediterranean cuisines, these plump, firm seeds have a nutty flavor and starchy, creamy texture that is perfect for roasting or blending into dips.

4
Once the pods and seeds have dried, pulses are ready to harvest. If they are harvested too early, then the seeds are too moist for storage.

5
At harvest time, the pods are plucked from the plants. The dry seeds are separated from the pods, and the pods are discarded.

6
The seeds are processed to ensure quality. Your pulses are cleaned, sorted, split, and milled before finding their way to store shelves and your table.

Kitchen-ready pulses

WHY EAT PULSES?

Pulses not only taste delicious, but they're also a smart choice for both your body and the world. These humble seeds boast substantial health benefits, and they are one of the most economical and sustainable sources of food.

THEY'RE GOOD FOR YOU

High in essential vitamins and minerals but low in fat, pulses are widely considered to be a superfood that can fight disease and contribute to a long, healthy life. Pulses are particularly good sources of fiber and protein, a pairing that provides sustained energy but keeps cholesterol levels low.

Beans, chickpeas, peas, and lentils contain between 20 and 25 percent protein by weight, much more than other popular plant-based protein sources, such as spinach and quinoa. This makes them an attractive alternative to meat-based proteins, particularly for vegans and vegetarians.

Pulses are also rich in key minerals like iron, potassium, zinc, and manganese, all of which play important roles in maintaining health.

Health benefits

Preserve heart health
Cholesterol-free and low in fat, pulses reduce the risk of heart disease.

Boost energy
Pulses are rich in iron, which helps transport oxygen in your bloodstream, rejuvenating your cells and your body.

Build strong bones
Dense in manganese and other important nutrients, pulses promote healthy bone structure.

Maintain the gut
Pulses are fiber-packed and high in prebiotics, your body's natural digestive regulators.

Improve brain function
High in folic acid, pulses can improve mental and emotional health.

Aid weight loss
Pulses contain amino acids that boost metabolism as well as soluble fiber to make you feel fuller, longer.

Control diabetes
Complex carbohydrates and a low Glycemic Index provide steady glucose release to regulate insulin in the blood.

per serving **CHICKPEAS** have **5X** more **IRON** than **SPINACH**

THEY'RE GOOD FOR THE PLANET

Not just good for your body, pulses are good for everybody. Pound for pound, they can feed more people than meat and require just a fraction of the resources required to raise livestock. Growing pulses also enriches the soil, improving crop yield.

Greater water efficiency

Pulse crops such as lentils and chickpeas are well-adapted to semi-arid climates and are more drought-tolerant than other crops, so they require less water than other plants and livestock. They also use water differently than other crops, drawing from the shallow depth of the soil and leaving the deeper-down water in place for the next year's growth.

Water used to produce one pound

Growing pulses is significantly more sustainable for the environment than managing livestock. Per pound, beef depletes 43 times more water than pulses.

pulses	soybeans	chicken	pork	beef
43 gallons	216 gallons	469 gallons	756 gallons	1857 gallons

Reduced carbon footprint

It takes energy to produce food, and that energy generates greenhouse gas emissions. But pulses are more eco-friendly than other foods because they require no nitrogen fertilizer. Nitrogen fertilizer uses energy-intensive production processes and emits nitrous oxide, which has nearly 300 times the global warming potential of carbon dioxide.

The water savings of growing **365 pounds** OF **PULSES** instead of beef would fill an **OLYMPIC SIZE POOL**

Increased food security

For many people, regular access to meat, dairy, and fish may be cost prohibitive. Pulses provide a safe and nutritious food at a low cost, and their long shelf life means they can be stored for months without losing nutritional value, reducing food waste.

Especially in developing countries, pulses can lift farmers out of rural poverty. Pulses can command prices two to three times higher than cereal crops, and their processing provides local job opportunities.

Higher crop yields

Farmers all across the world know how important pulses are to their sustainable farming systems. Unlike most crops, pulses extract nitrogen from the air around them and fix it to the soil, leaving behind nitrogen-rich residues and other compounds that help fight disease and insects. This enriches the soil, making it possible for the next crop in rotation to produce higher yields.

LENTILS

Lentil cultivation dates back to 7000 BCE, making it one of the world's oldest crops. Now they're grown and eaten on nearly every continent. They don't require pre-soaking, so they're an easy protein-packed supplement for plant-based diets.

GREEN LENTIL ▶

Also called Le Puy lentil, Lentilles du Puy, and French green lentil

The green lentil has a rich, deep flavor and holds its shape well after cooking. Use it in salads, stews, and casseroles to accentuate its firm texture.

Nutrition per ½ cup, cooked

Calories 115 Protein 9g
Carbohydrates 20g Fiber 8g

Good source of iron

Excellent source of fiber

◀ BROWN LENTIL

Varieties include Spanish pardina, German brown, Indian brown, and brewer lentil

The most common type of lentil, it ranges from a light khaki color to a deep, ruddy brown. This lentil has a creamy, slightly nutty taste that works in a variety of cuisines. Moderately firm, it can either hold its shape in soups and casseroles or mash easily for burgers and patties.

Nutrition per ½ cup, cooked

Calories 115 Protein 9g
Carbohydrates 20g Fiber 8g

Good source of potassium and vitamin B6

Excellent source of folate

◀ BELUGA LENTIL

Also called black lentil and petite beluga lentil

The shiny and small black pulse is named after the caviar it resembles. The beluga lentil is mild in flavor and holds its shape when cooked, making it a great ingredient for salads, pilafs, and stuffings.

Nutrition per ½ cup, cooked

Calories 90 **Protein** 7g
Carbohydrates 16g **Fiber** 8g

Good source of amino acids

Excellent source of protein

◀ YELLOW LENTIL

Also called golden lentil, toor dal, arhar dal, and tan lentils

Similar to red lentils, the yellow lentil is mild, sweet, and faintly nutty. It disintegrates quickly during cooking, which works well in spreads and soups. You'll often find yellow lentils in Indian dishes such as curries and dal.

Nutrition per ½ cup, cooked

Calories 115 **Protein** 9g
Carbohydrates 20g **Fiber** 8g

Good source of potassium

Excellent source of manganese

◀ RED LENTIL

Also called petite red lentil, crimson lentil, and red chief

Mild and slightly sweet, this lentil is pinkish-orange and sold both whole and split. Since it's very small, it breaks down quickly once cooked and is ideal for soups and dips. You can even use red lentils as a thickening agent for gravies and stews.

Nutrition per ½ cup, cooked

Calories 115 **Protein** 9g
Carbohydrates 20g **Fiber** 8g

Good source of slow-digesting carbohydrates and fiber

Excellent source of zinc and iron

	6OZ of LENTILS	VS.	6oz ground BEEF
calories	192	VS.	361
sat. fat	0g	VS.	10g
cholesterol	0mg	VS.	114mg
protein	18g	VS.	31g

BEANS

From the common to the exotic, there are many types of dried beans to explore and enjoy. Seek out unfamiliar varieties to experience the range of flavors and textures.

NAVY BEAN ▶

Also called pea bean, white pea bean, and pearl haricot bean

Small and creamy, the navy bean is slightly flattened and oval shaped. It's excellent for baked beans, soups, dips, and spreads. In addition to lots of heart-healthy protein, the navy bean is full of dietary fiber that helps stabilize blood sugar.

Nutrition per ½ cup, cooked

Calories 127 **Protein** 7g
Carbohydrates 24g **Fiber** 10g

Good source of copper and iron

Excellent source of iron, folate, and manganese

BLACK-EYED PEA ▲

Also called cowpea, California buckeye, and purple hull pea

Grown all over the world, the black-eyed pea usually dons a single, prominent spot before being cooked. It appears in salads, rice dishes, and soups and complements bold flavors.

Nutrition per ½ cup, cooked

Calories 100 **Protein** 7g
Carbohydrates 18g **Fiber** 7g

Good source of potassium

Excellent source of vitamin K

◀ ADZUKI BEAN

Also called azuki bean and aduki bean

Originating from Asia, this bean is small and burgundy. Its mild flavor lends the bean to sweet preparations; red bean paste is common in many Asian desserts. Also use it as you would the black bean in soups and chilis.

Nutrition per ½ cup, cooked

Calories 147 **Protein** 9g
Carbohydrates 28g **Fiber** 8g

Good source of folate, vitamin B6, protein, and fiber

Excellent source of phosphorous, zinc, and potassium

◄ PINTO BEAN

Also called speckled bean and strawberry bean

Spanish for "painted," this medium-sized bean is speckled beige and red. When cooked, the specks disappear and the bean turns bright pink. It's perfect for refried beans and chili.

Nutrition per ½ cup, cooked

Calories 122 **Protein** 8g
Carbohydrates 22g **Fiber** 8g

Good source of protein, phosphorous, and manganese

Excellent source of vitamin B1, vitamin B6, potassium, and iron

KIDNEY BEAN ▲

Also called red bean

This medium-sized red bean resembles a kidney in shape and color. It is commonly found both dried and canned and is often used in soups and chilis. High in fiber and protein, kidney beans contribute to a healthy heart.

Nutrition per ½ cup, cooked

Calories 112 **Protein** 8g
Carbohydrates 20g **Fiber** 7g

Good source of iron and folate

Excellent source of calcium

◄ LIMA BEAN

Also called butter bean and sieva bean

Dried lima beans are flat, kidney shaped, and white. The lima bean has a creamy texture, which lends it to inclusion in dips and traditional succotash recipes. Despite its rich texture, the lima bean is a nearly fat-free source of protein and fiber.

Nutrition per ½ cup, cooked

Calories 108 **Protein** 7g
Carbohydrates 20g **Fiber** 7g

Good source of folate and magnesium

Excellent source of soluble fiber

◄ BLACK BEAN

Also called black turtle bean

Shiny and black, this bean earns its nickname "turtle" because of its smooth shell exterior. The black bean's meaty texture and mild taste makes it perfect for vegetarian recipes. It's commonly found in soups and served with rice in many cultures.

Nutrition per ½ cup, cooked

Calories 127 **Protein** 7g
Carbohydrates 24g **Fiber** 10g

Good source of calcium, iron, and zinc

Excellent source of phytonutrients

◄ GREAT NORTHERN BEAN

Also called cannellini bean and white bean

This medium-sized flat bean has a creamy, off-white color. Its hearty texture makes it a natural addition to soups and stews, as well as braises and casseroles. It's an especially good substitute for the similar navy bean and an excellent source of protein and fiber.

Nutrition per ½ cup, cooked

Calories 127 **Protein** 8g
Carbohydrates 22g **Fiber** 6g

Good source of vitamin C and magnesium

Excellent source of phosphorous, iron, and potassium

CONTINUED ▶

◄ MUNG BEAN

Also called moong bean and green gram

This small, green pulse is used in both sweet and savory applications. It is commonly found in Indian and Asian cooking but can also easily be sprouted, usually called "bean sprouts" in recipes.

Nutrition per ½ cup, cooked

Calories 106 **Protein** 7g
Carbohydrates 19g **Fiber** 8g

Good source of fiber and protein

Excellent source of folate, magnesium, and vitamin B1

◄ SCARLET RUNNER

Also called runner bean and multiflora bean

Originally from Mexico, the scarlet runner bean is one of the oldest cultivated foods of the Americas. The large bean is a striking purple and black color and has a dense, meaty texture. It's easily used in stews, casseroles, and chilis.

Nutrition per ½ cup, cooked

Calories 166 **Protein** 9g
Carbohydrates 37g **Fiber** 15g

Good source of vitamin B1, niacin, and potassium

Excellent source of calcium and fiber

FLAGEOLET ▲

Varieties include chevrier and Flambeau

From France, this small, pale mint-green and kidney-shaped bean is an exquisite treat. Simple preparations, herbs, and dressings highlight the firm and creamy texture and mild taste.

Nutrition per ½ cup, cooked

Calories 300 **Protein** 20g
Carbohydrates 54g **Fiber** 22g

Good source of vitamin C

Excellent source of fiber

BORLOTTI BEAN ►

Also called cranberry bean, Roman bean, saluggia bean, and rosecoco bean

Tender, moist, and beautifully speckled when dry, the borlotti bean turns brown when cooked. It is plump, bittersweet, and excellent for vegetable stews, casseroles, and salads.

Nutrition per ½ cup, cooked

Calories 90 **Protein** 6g
Carbohydrates 16g **Fiber** 8g

Good source of phosphorous

Excellent source of iron

◀ MOTH BEAN

Also called moath bean, moat bean, matki, mat bean, and Turkish gram

Cultivated in many parts of the world, from India to Italy, the moth bean is a small, light brown cylindrical pulse with a nutty flavor. Its flavor profile complements aromatic spices, coconut, and foods with a touch of sweetness.

Nutrition per ½ cup, cooked

Calories 104 **Protein** 7g
Carbohydrates 18g **Fiber** 8g

Good source of iron and magnesium

Excellent source of folate

FAVA BEAN ▲

Also called faba bean, broad bean

The long-cultivated fava bean is meaty, earthy, buttery, and bold. After soaking, most cooks prefer to pop each fava bean out of its skin before cooking. Though large, it disintegrates quickly, making it a great candidate to purée or mash.

Nutrition per ½ cup, cooked

Calories 168 **Protein** 16g
Carbohydrates 22g **Fiber** 16g

Good source of phosphorous, copper, and manganese

Excellent source of folate

BLACK GRAM ▲

Also called vinga mungo, black lentil, black urad dal, and mungo bean

Most often used in Indian cooking, the black gram is a small, black cylindrical pulse with a creamy white interior. The deep, earthy flavor makes it a perfect match for curries, stews, and other boldly flavored dishes.

Nutrition per ½ cup, cooked

Calories 115 **Protein** 9g
Carbohydrates 20g **Fiber** 8g

Good source of magnesium

Excellent source of iron, folic acid, and calcium

HEIRLOOM BEANS

Untouched by genetic science, there are endless varieties of heirloom beans, each with a unique look and depth of flavor. They are cultivated in a single setting for generations, never mass-produced, so the genetic pureness produces the same seed with each generation of planting. Heirlooms are not usually on the shelves of ordinary stores, but when you do find them, they are a culinary delight.

Orca bean

CHICKPEAS

There are two main types of chickpeas—desi and kabuli. The desi is small and dark, but the more common kabuli is larger and paler, usually just labeled "chickpea" at the store.

PEAS

Unlike peanuts and fresh peas, dry peas are low in fat and harvested dry. Pigeon peas and split peas are most common, but you can also find green and yellow dry peas in whole form.

◄ PIGEON PEA

Also called split toor dal

Nutty and crisp, the pigeon pea is a key food source around the world—hearty, drought resistant, and cultivated for over 3,000 years. The small, glossy brown pea is often served alongside rice for a complete meal.

Nutrition per ½ cup, cooked

Calories 126 **Protein** 7g
Carbohydrates 22g
Fiber 7g

Good source of folate

Excellent source of magnesium

CHICKPEA ▲

Also called garbanzo bean, gram, Bengal gram, chana dal, kabuli

This domesticated chickpea dates to mesolithic cultures. The chickpea—though not actually a true pea—has a nutty flavor and creamy texture. The soft, starchy quality makes it versatile for dips, salads, spreads, and curries.

Nutrition per ½ cup, cooked

Calories 134 **Protein** 8g
Carbohydrates 22g **Fiber** 6g

Good source of antioxidants

Excellent source of fiber

SPLIT PEA ►

Varieties include green split pea and yellow split pea

The split pea is harvested whole then split in half. It is similar in taste and texture to lentils but rounder in shape and brighter in color. It's best known for making soups and Indian dal, but also works well in dips and spreads.

Nutrition per ½ cup, cooked

Calories 116 **Protein** 8g
Carbohydrates 20g **Fiber** 8g

Good source of vitamin A

Excellent source of low-fat protein

PULSE FLOURS

Almost any pulse can be ground into a flour, but white beans, chickpeas, and black beans are most common. They don't contain gluten, so they're an excellent addition to allergy-sensitive diets.

Pulse flours taste different from traditional wheat flour, each with a unique flavor profile. Use them for baking, soups, dips, and breading, as well as binders and thickeners. Substituting some or all of the wheat flour in recipes with a pulse flour adds extra nutrition to your baking and cooking. When used for baking, you'll need to combine pulse flours with another gluten-free or traditional wheat flour to help mixtures rise.

◄ WHITE BEAN FLOUR

This flour is extremely mild. When combined with stabilizers such as Xanthan gum or potato starch, white bean flour is an excellent substitute in gluten-free baking. The creamy mild texture makes it a natural addition to soups, sauces, and gravies.

Nutrition per ½ cup

Calories 110 **Protein** 7g
Carbohydrates 20g **Fiber** 8g

Good source of folate and manganese

Excellent source of phosphorous

▲ CHICKPEA FLOUR

This is one of the most versatile pulse flours. It's creamy, sweet, and slightly nutty, making chickpea flour a great addition to baked goods and pizza crust. Use it in recipes that contain bold flavors like pumpkin bread or Middle Eastern fare.

Nutrition per ½ cup

Calories 110 **Protein** 6g
Carbohydrates 18g **Fiber** 5g

Good source of iron

Excellent source of dietary fiber

BLACK BEAN FLOUR ►

Ground from black turtle beans, black bean flour has a deep, rich, earthy flavor. It's sometimes simply mixed with water and served as a dip, but it can also be used a thickener or filling in Mexican recipes.

Nutrition per ½ cup

Calories 120 **Protein** 8g
Carbohydrates 22g **Fiber** 5g

Good source of dietary fiber

Excellent source of low-fat protein

HOW TO COOK PULSES

Cooking dried pulses rewards you with depth of flavor and control of variables like consistency and sodium. The stovetop is the most common method to cook pulses, but you can also use a slow cooker or pressure cooker.

1 PREPARE

Sort the pulses on a tray, removing broken and irregular pieces as well as foreign items, like small stones. Then remove dirt and grit by rinsing the pulses in a fine mesh sieve.

2 SOAK

Place pulses in a large bowl and cover with cool water about 2 inches (5cm) above the level of the pulses. Most should soak for 8 hours or overnight.

3 DRAIN & RINSE

Drain and rinse again in a fine mesh sieve under cool water to wash away impurities or toxins released by soaking.

4 COOK

Transfer pulses to a stockpot. Cover with water at least 2 inches (5cm) above the level of the pulses. Bring to a boil then reduce to a simmer and cook per the pulse's cooking time (see page 23). Periodically skim off any foam that develops on the surface.

5 CHECK

For a perfectly cooked batch, check on your pulses within the suggested cooking time range by pinching and tasting a few from the pot.

Perfect
A perfectly cooked, tender pulse will yield easily when pinched and is soft throughout while maintaining its shape.

Undercooked
An undercooked pulse is too firm and will not give when pinched, indicating that it needs more cooking time.

Overcooked
An overcooked pulse is mushy and loses its shape, but you can still salvage the batch for dips, spreads, and purées.

Adding flavor

For a robust flavor profile, use stock instead of water and add bay leaves, onions, garlic, and other aromatics to the cooking liquid. However, don't add salt until the last half hour of cooking. Salt added too early can toughen the skins and prolong cooking time.

Batch cooking & freezing

Most cooked pulse varieties freeze well, making it easy to keep them on hand. Let cooked pulses dry and cool completely, then portion into airtight plastic freezer bags. They will keep safely in the refrigerator for up to 3 days or in the freezer for several months without losing nutritional value.

Using canned beans

Canned beans can be used in place of home-cooked beans in any recipe. Be sure to thoroughly rinse them before using because the packaging liquid can nearly double the sodium content. A 15-ounce (425g) can contains about 1½ cups of beans.

Many recipes work equally well with home-cooked or canned pulses.

SPROUTING

Sprouted pulses are fresh, crisp, and bursting with nutrients. Before getting started, be sure to select a pulse variety that is suitable for sprouting.

1 In a large jar, generously cover pulses with water. Cover the mouth of the jar with cheesecloth and secure. Soak in a cool, dark place for 8 hours or overnight.

2 Drain the jar. Run fresh water through to rinse the pulses once or twice. Then tip the jar sideways and let the water completely drain.

3 Return to the storage space on its side with the base elevated to allow pulses to sprout. About every 12 hours, repeat step 2 then return to the storage space.

4 When sprouts reach the desired length, remove from the jar and dry. Most varieties require 2 to 4 days to reach an average length. Store in an airtight bag or a container in the refrigerator.

PERFECTLY PREPARED

Some pulses require soaking and long simmers, others cook more quickly, and many are perfect to sprout for fresh texture or swap into your favorite recipes.

		Soak time	Stovetop simmer time	Pressure cooker time (on high)	Slow cooker time (on low)	Suitable for sprouting	Good substitutes
PEAS	Pigeon pea	8 hrs–overnight	45 mins–1 hr	6–9 mins	2–3 hrs	✸	Black-eyed pea
	Split pea	Not required	30 mins	1 min	6–8 hrs		Green lentil
LENTILS	Beluga lentil	Not required	25 mins	1 min	6–7 hrs	✸	Brown lentil, green lentil
	Brown lentil	Not required	20–25 mins	1 min	6–7 hrs	✸	Beluga lentil, green lentil
	Green lentil	Not required	20–25 mins	1 min	6–7 hrs	✸	Beluga lentil, brown lentil
	Red lentil	Not required	15–20 mins	1 min	6–7 hrs	✸	Yellow lentil
	Yellow lentil	Not required	15–20 mins	1 min	6–7 hrs	✸	Red lentil
BEANS	Adzuki bean	1–2 hrs	45 mins–1 hr	5–9 mins	6–8 hrs	✸	Mung bean
	Black bean	8 hrs–overnight	45 mins–1 hr	9–11 mins	6–8 hrs		Borlotti bean, pinto bean, navy bean
	Black-eyed pea	8 hrs–overnight	1 hr	3–5 mins	6–8 hrs	✸	Pigeon pea
	Black gram	8 hrs–overnight	30 mins	7 mins	6–8 hrs		Moth bean
	Borlotti bean	8 hrs–overnight	1hr–90 mins	7–10 mins	6–7 hrs		Great Northern bean, pinto bean
	Chickpea	8 hrs–overnight	1hr–90 mins	10–12 mins	6–8 hrs	✸	Great Northern bean
	Fava bean	8 hrs–overnight	1–2 hrs	10–12 mins	3–4 hrs		Yellow split pea
	Flageolet	8 hrs–overnight	1–90 mins	6–8 mins	6–7 hrs		Great Northern bean, navy bean
	Great Northern bean	8 hrs–overnight	1 hr	8–12 mins	6–8 hrs		Navy bean
	Kidney bean	8 hrs–overnight	1–90 mins	6–8 mins	6–7 hrs		Great Northern bean
	Lima bean	8 hrs–overnight	1 hr	4–7 mins	6–7 hrs		Navy bean
	Moth bean	8 hrs–overnight	20–25 mins	5–6 mins	4–6 hrs	✸	Black gram, beluga lentil
	Mung bean	Not required	30–45 mins	5–9 mins	6–8 hrs	✸	Adzuki bean
	Navy bean	8 hrs–overnight	1–90 mins	6–8 mins	6–7 hrs		Great Northern bean
	Pinto bean	8 hrs–overnight	1 hr–75 mins	4–6 mins	6–7 hrs		Kidney bean, borlotti bean
	Scarlet runner	8 hrs–overnight	90 mins	5–8 mins	5–7 hrs		Kidney bean

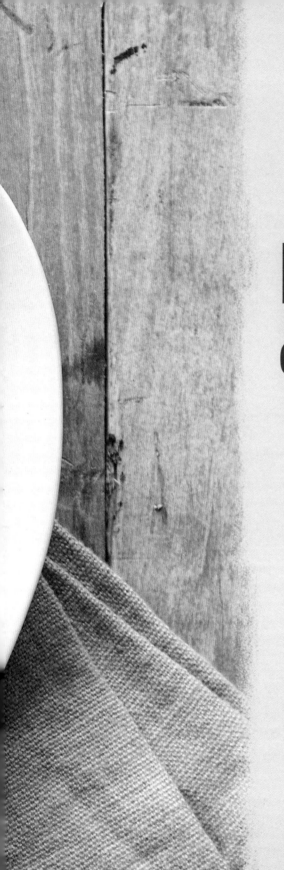

BREAKFAST & BRUNCH

CURRIED MUNG BEAN AVOCADO TOAST

Sprouts and mung beans elevate avocado toast to the next level of tasty. The hint of curry flavor works well with the creamy, smooth avocado.

MAKES 3 · PREP 10 MINS · COOK 4 MINS

3 slices sourdough or
  whole-wheat country bread
1 ripe avocado
1 cup cooked mung beans
½ tsp curry powder
Pinch turmeric
Salt and pepper
¾ cup sprouted mung beans
3 tbsp chopped chives

1 In a skillet over medium-low heat, toast slices of bread for 2 minutes on each side, or until brown and crisp. Remove from the skillet and let cool slightly.

2 Cut avocado in half and remove pit. Scoop out flesh of one half and add to a medium mixing bowl. With a potato masher, mash avocado half.

3 Stir in mung beans, curry powder, and turmeric. Taste and season with salt and pepper. Spread avocado mixture evenly over slices of toast.

4 Remove flesh from remaining avocado half and thinly slice. Arrange equal amounts atop each slice of toast.

5 Place on serving plates and sprinkle with equal amounts sprouted mung beans and chives. Serve immediately.

Nutrition per toast

Calories	330
Total Fat	9g
Saturated Fat	1.5g
Cholesterol	0mg
Sodium	340mg
Total Carbohydrate	53g
Dietary Fiber	9g
Sugars	4g
Protein	14g

● **Make it with meat**
Crumble 2 slices cooked bacon into avocado–mung bean mixture.

LENTIL CREAM CHEESE TARTINES

Flavored cream cheese is so easy to make at home. Adding lentils, chives, and lemon zest to the rich spread creates great texture and protein for the simple breakfast dish.

MAKES 6 · PREP 5 MINS · COOK 25 MINS

6 slices whole-wheat bread

8oz (225g) cream cheese, softened

¾ cup cooked brown lentils

2 tbsp chopped chives

Zest 1 lemon

Salt and pepper

3 tsp olive oil

6 large eggs

2 cups watercress

1 Preheat the oven to 300°F (150°C). Arrange slices of bread on a baking sheet. Toast for 5 minutes, flip, and toast for another 5 minutes until crisp and golden.

2 Meanwhile, to make cream cheese spread, in a food processor blend cream cheese, lentils, chives, and lemon zest until thoroughly combined. Season with salt and pepper to taste. Spread cream cheese mixture evenly over slices of toast.

3 In a nonstick skillet, heat 1 teaspoon oil over medium-low heat until shimmering. Crack 2 eggs into the skillet and cook for 2 to 3 minutes until whites are set but yolks are runny. Place each cooked egg atop a slice of toast then repeat with remaining 4 eggs. Top each tartine with ⅓ cup watercress and serve immediately.

Nutrition per tartine

Calories	280
Total Fat	17g
Saturated Fat	8g
Cholesterol	40mg
Sodium	400mg
Total Carbohydrate	22g
Dietary Fiber	4g
Sugars	4g
Protein	13g

● **Make it with meat**

Top each tartine with 1 ounce (28g) smoked salmon, thinly sliced.

ROASTED TOMATO & CHICKPEA FRITTATA

Frittatas are a wonderful way to feed a crowd for breakfast or brunch. Chickpeas add an unexpected twist and extra body to this morning classic.

SERVES 10 · PREP 15 MINS · COOK 30 MINS

1 dry pint (473g) grape
   tomatoes

1 garlic clove, minced

2 thyme sprigs

1 tbsp olive oil

10 large eggs

2 tbsp heavy cream

2 tsp chopped chives

Salt and pepper

3 cups baby spinach

2 cups cooked chickpeas

1 Preheat the oven to 400°F (200°C). On a rimmed baking sheet, toss tomatoes, garlic, and thyme in oil. Spread in an even layer and roast for 10 minutes. Discard thyme sprigs. Let cool slightly.

2 Meanwhile, in a large mixing bowl, whisk together eggs, heavy cream, and chives. Season with salt and pepper to taste.

3 Heat a 10-inch (25cm) cast-iron or ovenproof skillet over medium heat. Transfer tomatoes to the skillet. Add spinach and cook for 1 to 2 minutes until spinach slightly wilts. Add chickpeas and stir to combine. Spread mixture evenly across the skillet.

4 Pour egg mixture over tomatoes, spinach, and chickpeas. Cook uncovered on the stovetop for 2 to 3 minutes until edges of egg begin to set. Transfer the skillet to the oven and cook uncovered for an additional 8 to 10 minutes until edges are set but center is still slightly springy. Serve immediately.

● **Make it with meat**

Add 5 ounces (140g) finely diced ham or chicken sausage, cooked, to the skillet with chickpeas in step 3.

Nutrition per serving

Calories	130
Total Fat	8g
Saturated Fat	2.5g
Cholesterol	190mg
Sodium	360mg
Total Carbohydrate	7g
Dietary Fiber	2g
Sugars	2g
Protein	8g

Why not try…

For a creamy tang, sprinkle 4 ounces (110g) goat cheese over egg mixture before baking.

COCONUT, DATE, & MOTH BEAN GRANOLA

Toasting the moth beans in this recipe makes them take on a dark color and deeply sweet, caramelized taste. Their nutty flavor complements the sweetness of the dates and coconut.

SERVES 8 · PREP 20 MINS · COOK 50 MINS

1 ½ cups cooked moth beans

2 tbsp coconut oil

½ cup agave nectar

1 tsp vanilla extract

1 tsp cinnamon

1 cup roughly chopped almonds

½ cup roasted sunflower seeds

⅔ cup pitted and chopped dates

⅔ cup unsweetened coconut flakes

1 Preheat the oven to 325°F (180°C). Spread moth beans on a light-colored, rimmed baking sheet and let dry for 5 minutes while you measure remaining ingredients. Then transfer the sheet to the oven and toast moth beans for 3 to 5 minutes until lightly crispy.

2 On the baking sheet, toss toasted moth beans with coconut oil, agave, vanilla, and cinnamon. Arrange in a single layer, return to the oven, and bake for 6 to 8 minutes.

3 On the baking sheet, incorporate almonds and sunflower seeds. Bake for an additional 20 to 30 minutes until mixture is toasted but not burnt, stirring occasionally.

4 Stir in dates and coconut flakes. Return to the oven and bake for up to 5 additional minutes until all ingredients are toasted and crunchy, stirring as needed. Remove from the oven and let sit for 10 minutes before serving. Store in an airtight container in the refrigerator for up to 3 days.

Nutrition per serving

Calories	230
Total Fat	14g
Saturated Fat	5g
Cholesterol	185mg
Sodium	0mg
Total Carbohydrate	24g
Dietary Fiber	6g
Sugars	13g
Protein	7g

Pulse exchange

Substitute an equal amount **black gram** or **beluga lentils** for moth beans.

PEANUT & RED LENTIL GRANOLA BARS

These granola bars are a versatile, portable, and good-for-you homemade snack.

MAKES 10 · PREP 15 MINS, PLUS 3 HRS TO SET

⅔ cup cooked red lentils

1 ½ cups rolled oats

4 tbsp honey

¼ cup chia seeds

2 tbsp coconut oil

⅓ cup roughly chopped almonds

⅓ tsp cinnamon

2 tsp vanilla extract

½ cup creamy peanut butter

⅓ cup semi-sweet chocolate chips, optional

1 Line an 8x8-inch (20x20cm) baking pan with parchment paper and set aside.

2 In a large mixing bowl, combine lentils, oats, honey, chia seeds, coconut oil, almonds, cinnamon, vanilla, and peanut butter. If using, gently fold in chocolate chips.

3 Transfer mixture to the baking pan and spread evenly. Cover the pan with aluminum foil or plastic wrap and refrigerate for 3 hours or overnight.

4 Use the parchment lining to remove mixture from the pan. Cut the square in half then cut each half into 5 pieces, making 10 bars total. Store in an airtight container in the refrigerator for up to 4 days.

● **Make it vegan**

Rather than honey, substitute an equal amount agave nectar.

Nutrition per bar

Calories	220
Total Fat	12g
Saturated Fat	4g
Cholesterol	0mg
Sodium	60mg
Total Carbohydrate	23g
Dietary Fiber	4g
Sugars	9g
Protein	7g

Why not try... Add ¼ cup dried cranberries or chopped dates rather than chocolate chips.

CINNAMON RAISIN BREAKFAST QUINOA

Quinoa and lentils can be breakfast food, too. With the warm flavors of vanilla, cinnamon, and almond, this dish is as comforting as oatmeal but with more protein and fiber.

SERVES 6 · PREP 10 MINS · COOK 35 MINS

1 cup dry quinoa

1 large vanilla bean

4 cups unsweetened almond milk

¼ cup agave nectar or honey

1 cinnamon stick

¼ tsp ground nutmeg

½ cup dry yellow lentils

1 cup raisins

1 cup chopped almonds

1 Place quinoa in a fine mesh strainer and rinse thoroughly. Let air dry slightly.

2 Meanwhile, cut vanilla bean down the middle lengthwise. Scrape out vanilla seeds. Reserve both seeds and pod.

3 In a medium saucepan, combine almond milk, agave, cinnamon stick, nutmeg, and vanilla seeds and pod. Bring to a gentle boil. Add quinoa and lentils. Cook, covered, for 20 to 25 minutes until lentils and quinoa are tender and most liquid is absorbed. Remove vanilla pod and cinnamon stick.

4 To serve, portion into six bowls. Drizzle with additional almond milk if desired, and top each bowl with equal amounts raisins and chopped almonds.

Pulse exchange

Instead of yellow lentils, use an equal amount **red lentils.**

Nutrition per serving

Calories	410
Total Fat	13g
Saturated Fat	1g
Cholesterol	0mg
Sodium	110mg
Total Carbohydrate	65g
Dietary Fiber	7g
Sugars	29g
Protein	13g

CHICKPEA & ROOT VEGETABLE HASH

This breakfast hash elevates simple root vegetables and makes them the star. A luscious egg yolk creates a rich sauce for the roasted vegetables.

SERVES 6 · PREP 20 MINS · COOK 30 MINS

2 tbsp coconut oil

1 small sweet potato, peeled and diced

1 medium turnip, peeled and diced

1 large parsnip, peeled and diced

3 carrots, diced

1 tbsp thyme

Pinch red pepper flakes

½ tsp ancho chili powder

2 cups cooked chickpeas

Salt and pepper

6 large eggs

1 Preheat the oven to 375°F (190°C). In a large cast-iron skillet, heat oil over medium heat. Once shimmering, add sweet potato, turnip, parsnip, and carrots. Stir to coat.

2 Add thyme, red pepper flakes, and ancho chili powder. Stir once more, then place the skillet in the oven and cook for 20 minutes until vegetables are tender. Remove from the oven, add chickpeas, stir, and return to the oven. Cook for 5 additional minutes until chickpeas are warmed through.

3 Meanwhile, heat a large nonstick skillet over medium heat. Crack one egg into the skillet and cook for 3 minutes, or until white is set but yolk is runny. Remove and repeat for remaining 5 eggs.

4 Taste and season hash with salt and pepper. Divide between 6 serving plates and top each with an egg. Serve immediately.

● Make it with meat

Sauté ⅛ cup diced pancetta in coconut oil before adding root vegetables.

Pulse exchange

If you don't have chickpeas, use an equal amount **adzuki beans** or **navy beans**.

Nutrition per serving

Calories	260
Total Fat	11g
Saturated Fat	6g
Cholesterol	185mg
Sodium	320mg
Total Carbohydrate	28g
Dietary Fiber	7g
Sugars	7g
Protein	12g

YELLOW LENTIL BERRY SMOOTHIE

Having cooked lentils on hand is an easy and undetectable way to quickly add protein—and a boost of rich color—to your three berry smoothie.

MAKES 2 · PREP 10 MINS

2 cups sliced strawberries
½ cup blueberries
½ cup blackberries
⅓ cup cooked yellow lentils
2 tbsp agave nectar
1 cup milk

1 In a blender, combine strawberries, blueberries, blackberries, lentils, agave, and milk.

2 Blend until fully combined, then pour into two glasses and serve immediately.

● Make
it vegan

Instead of milk, substitute vanilla almond milk or coconut milk.

Pulse exchange
Rather than yellow lentils, substitute an equal amount **green lentils** or **brown lentils**.

Nutrition per smoothie

Calories	229
Total Fat	3g
Saturated Fat	0g
Cholesterol	0mg
Sodium	49mg
Total Carbohydrate	46g
Dietary Fiber	8g
Sugars	31g
Protein	8g

BLACK BEAN BREAKFAST TOSTADAS

These crunchy fried tortillas are topped with creamy scrambled eggs and spicy seasoned black beans for an irresistible and savory breakfast.

MAKES 4 · PREP 15 MINS · COOK 20 MINS

1 tbsp olive oil

1 small white onion, finely diced

1 jalapeño, deseeded and finely diced

1 garlic clove, minced

2 cups cooked black beans

1 tbsp ground cumin

1 tsp chipotle chili powder

½ cup vegetable stock

Salt and pepper

4 corn tostada shells

4 large eggs

½ tbsp heavy cream

4oz (110g) Cotija cheese

Cilantro, to garnish

Hot sauce, to garnish

1 Preheat the oven to 325°F (170°C). In a medium skillet, heat oil over medium-low heat. Add onion and cook for 5 minutes, or until translucent. Add jalapeño and garlic and cook for an additional 2 to 3 minutes.

2 Add black beans, cumin, and chipotle chili powder and stir to coat. Add stock, bring to boil, then reduce to a simmer and cook for 5 minutes, or until liquid reduces. Taste and season with salt and pepper.

3 Meanwhile, on a rimmed baking sheet, arrange tostada shells in an even layer with edges slightly overlapping. Bake for 2 to 3 minutes until warmed through.

4 In a small mixing bowl, whisk together eggs and heavy cream. In a nonstick skillet over medium-low heat, scramble eggs to desired consistency.

5 To assemble, spread equal amounts black bean mixture on tostada shells. Top with equal amounts scrambled eggs. Sprinkle 1 ounce (25g) Cotija cheese on each tostada, then garnish with fresh cilantro and hot sauce. Serve immediately.

Make it vegan

Instead of eggs, scramble 8 ounces (225g) firm tofu with salt and pepper.

Make it with meat

Crumble 1 slice cooked, crisp bacon over black beans as you assemble.

Nutrition per tostada

Calories	430
Total Fat	22g
Saturated Fat	8g
Cholesterol	220mg
Sodium	500mg
Total Carbohydrate	37g
Dietary Fiber	9g
Sugars	3g
Protein	21g

Why not try...

For a boost of healthy fats, top each tostada with wedges of sliced avocado.

SPICY MUNG BEAN SCRAMBLE

Mung beans have a mild taste and creamy texture—they're the perfect addition to this spicy bell pepper and jalapeño scramble.

● Make it with meat

Add any combination chopped, cooked meat—bacon, chicken, turkey, or ham. Add up to 1 ounce (25g) per serving along with mung beans.

SERVES 4 · PREP 15 MINS · COOK 15 MINS

1 tbsp olive oil

1 medium orange or yellow bell pepper, diced

2 green onions, chopped

1 small jalapeño, deseeded and minced

½ cup cooked mung beans

6 large eggs

Salt and pepper

Dash smoked paprika

1 ripe avocado, thinly sliced

½ cup chopped cilantro

¼ cup sprouted mung beans, optional

Hot sauce, to serve

1 In a medium nonstick skillet, heat oil over medium-low heat. Add bell pepper, green onion, and jalapeño and cook for 3 to 4 minutes until soft. Stir in mung beans and cook for an additional 1 to 2 minutes until warmed through.

2 Meanwhile, in a medium mixing bowl, whisk together eggs, salt and pepper to taste, and paprika. Pour egg mixture into the skillet with cooked vegetables. With a silicone spatula or wooden spoon, stir eggs until soft curds begin to form. Continue to cook eggs, stirring frequently, for 4 to 5 minutes over medium-low heat to preferred doneness. Remove from heat.

3 To serve, divide scrambled eggs among four plates. Garnish with a quarter each of sliced avocado and chopped cilantro. If using, sprinkle sprouted mung beans over top. Serve immediately, with hot sauce on the side.

Nutrition per serving

Calories	260
Total Fat	19g
Saturated Fat	4g
Cholesterol	280mg
Sodium	280mg
Total Carbohydrate	12g
Dietary Fiber	6g
Sugars	4g
Protein	13g

Why not try...

For a creamier texture, sprinkle in ⅓ cup shredded sharp cheddar or pepper jack cheese midway through cooking eggs.

ENGLISH BREAKFAST EGG-IN-THE-HOLE

This mash-up of the traditional English breakfast and egg-in-the-hole is an unexpected way to unite the two breakfast classics.

● **Make it with meat**

For a traditional English breakfast, add 1 bacon slice or 1 sausage link to each plate.

SERVES 4 · PREP 20 MINS · COOK 35 MINS

1 tbsp olive oil

1 small yellow onion, finely diced

1 garlic clove, minced

2 cups cooked navy beans

1 ¼ cups tomato purée

2 tbsp molasses

Pinch red pepper flakes

Salt and pepper

2 Roma tomatoes, halved lengthwise

2 cups quartered white mushrooms

4 slices whole-wheat bread

4 large eggs

1 To make baked beans, in a medium saucepan, heat oil over medium-low heat. Add onion and cook for 2 minutes. Add garlic and cook for an additional minute.

2 Stir in navy beans, tomato purée, molasses, and red pepper flakes. Bring to a boil then reduce to a simmer and cook for 20 minutes. Taste and season with salt and pepper.

3 Meanwhile, heat a large nonstick skillet over medium heat. Sear tomatoes, cut-side down, for 3 to 4 minutes until lightly cooked. Remove and set aside on serving plates. Then add mushrooms to the skillet. Season with salt and pepper and cook for 3 to 4 minutes until tender. Remove and place on the serving plates. Wipe out the skillet and return to the stove over medium-low heat.

4 With a 2-inch (5cm) diameter round cookie cutter, cut a hole from the middle of each slice of bread. Place two slices of bread, along with cut-out circles, in the skillet. Toast for 2 minutes, then flip over. Crack one egg into each hole and cook for 3 to 5 minutes until whites are set and yolks are cooked to desired doneness. Remove from the skillet and repeat for the remaining two slices of bread and eggs.

5 Place each egg-in-the-hole on a serving plate and top with baked beans. Serve each with roasted tomato half and sautéed mushrooms.

Nutrition per serving

Calories	380
Total Fat	10g
Saturated Fat	2.5g
Cholesterol	185mg
Sodium	230mg
Total Carbohydrate	54g
Dietary Fiber	14g
Sugars	15g
Protein	20g

ASPARAGUS & GREEN LENTILS
WITH POACHED EGG

● Make it
with meat

Add 1 slice crisped
prosciutto or bacon
to each plate.

This impressive-looking brunch dish couldn't be easier to
prepare. The yolk from the poached egg makes a luxurious
sauce over the roasted asparagus and lentils.

SERVES 4 · PREP 10 MINS · COOK 15 MINS

1 lb (450g) thin asparagus,
  woody ends trimmed

2 tbsp olive oil

Salt and pepper

2 ½ tbsp red wine vinegar

1 tbsp Dijon mustard

¼ tsp chopped thyme

Dash white vinegar

1 ⅓ cups cooked green lentils

4 large eggs

1 Preheat the oven to 350°F (180°C). Toss asparagus with
1 tablespoon oil. Arrange on a baking sheet in a single
layer and season with salt and pepper. Roast for 10 minutes,
or until tender.

2 Meanwhile, to make dressing, in a medium bowl combine
red wine vinegar, Dijon mustard, thyme, and remaining
1 tablespoon oil. Whisk until emulsified. Add lentils and stir
to combine. Set aside and let lentils absorb dressing.

3 To poach eggs, fill a large saucepan with water, about
1 ½-inches (4cm) deep. Bring water to a boil then reduce
to a simmer. Add white vinegar. One at a time, crack eggs
into a ramekin and gently tip egg into water. Cook for
3 minutes. Remove and place on a plate lined with paper
towel to absorb water.

4 To serve, divide asparagus among 4 plates and top each
with dressed lentils. Place one poached egg atop lentils.
Season with pepper and serve immediately.

Nutrition per serving

Calories	238
Total Fat	12.5g
Saturated Fat	2.6g
Cholesterol	183mg
Sodium	195mg
Total Carbohydrate	19g
Dietary Fiber	6g
Sugars	3.7g
Protein	15g

Pulse
exchange
Substitute an equal
amount **brown lentils** or
mung beans for
green lentils.

RED LENTIL SHAKSHUKA

This comforting, one-skillet meal is a traditional Mediterranean and easy-to-make breakfast of eggs baked in spicy tomato sauce. The red lentils add a hearty texture and nutty taste.

SERVES 4 · PREP 25 MINS · COOK 30 MINS

2 tbsp olive oil

1 small yellow onion, diced

1 red bell pepper, deseeded and chopped

2 garlic cloves, minced

1 Thai red chile, deseeded and minced

14oz (400g) can petite diced tomatoes

14oz (400g) can crushed tomatoes

1 tbsp tomato paste

1 tsp ground cumin

¾ tsp smoked paprika

2 tbsp red wine vinegar

¼ cup dry red lentils

Salt and pepper

4 large eggs

3 tbsp chopped flat-leaf parsley

1 In a 10-inch (25cm) cast-iron skillet, warm oil over medium-low heat until shimmering. Add onion and bell pepper and cook for 5 minutes, or until soft. Add garlic and chile and continue to cook for 1 to 2 minutes until fragrant.

2 Add diced tomatoes, crushed tomatoes, tomato paste, cumin, paprika, and vinegar and stir to combine. Cook for 5 minutes, or until warmed through. Add lentils and cook, covered, for 20 to 25 minutes until tender. Season with salt and pepper to taste.

3 With the back of a spoon, press to create 4 wells in tomato-lentil mixture in the skillet. Crack one egg into each well. Cover the skillet and cook for 5 to 8 minutes until eggs are just set. Sprinkle with parsley and serve immediately.

Nutrition per serving

Calories	240
Total Fat	12g
Saturated Fat	2.5g
Cholesterol	185mg
Sodium	280mg
Total Carbohydrate	21g
Dietary Fiber	5g
Sugars	8g
Protein	11g

● **Make it vegan**

Omit eggs and use tofu rounds, firmly pressed and cut into 4 ½-inch (11cm) slices.

MASCARPONE STUFFED FRENCH TOAST

The creamy, tangy filling of this decadent French toast is perfectly complemented by the bright citrus notes of the blood orange sauce.

MAKES 4 · PREP 30 MINS · COOK 30 MINS

● **Make it vegan**

Use 1 tablespoon chickpea flour and 3 tablespoons water, mixed, rather than egg, and replace Mascarpone with a vegan cheese alternative.

- 2 cups cooked Great Northern beans
- 2 tbsp granulated sugar
- 6oz (170g) Mascarpone cheese, softened
- ½ tbsp plus 1 tsp vanilla extract
- Zest 2 large blood oranges
- ½ cup agave nectar
- ½ cup blood orange juice (juice 4 small blood oranges)
- 1 tsp cornstarch
- 1 tbsp unsalted butter
- 1 large egg
- ¾ cup unsweetened almond milk
- ¼ tsp cinnamon
- Pinch salt
- 1 (14–16oz; 400–450g) loaf challah bread
- Powdered sugar, to garnish

1 To make filling, in a food processor, combine Great Northern beans, sugar, Mascarpone, ½ tablespoon vanilla, and blood orange zest. Pulse until thoroughly combined. Transfer to a small bowl and refrigerate at least one hour or overnight.

2 To make blood orange sauce, in a small saucepan, whisk together agave, blood orange juice, and cornstarch until smooth. Gently boil for 3 to 4 minutes until slightly thickened. Remove from heat and stir in butter.

3 To make batter, in a large mixing bowl or pie pan, whisk together egg, almond milk, cinnamon, and salt. Set aside.

4 Cut the narrow ends from challah to create an even loaf. Cut loaf into 4 (2-inch; 5cm) slices. To create pockets for filling, with a small knife cut a slit into the center of each slice without cutting fully through. Stuff each slice with 2 heaping tablespoons filling and press the cut to seal. Dredge each slice in batter for 1 minute on each side.

5 Heat a nonstick skillet over medium heat. In batches, cook slices for 2 to 3 minutes on each side until golden brown. Garnish with powdered sugar, top with blood orange sauce, and serve immediately.

Nutrition per French toast

Calories	650
Total Fat	19g
Saturated Fat	140g
Cholesterol	95mg
Sodium	670mg
Total Carbohydrate	98g
Dietary Fiber	9g
Sugars	29g
Protein	22g

Pulse exchange

Use an equal amount **flageolet beans** instead of Great Northern beans.

YELLOW LENTIL EGG MUFFINS

These cheesy egg muffins with sweet broccoli florets are an easy grab-and-go breakfast.

MAKES 12 · PREP 15 MINS · COOK 30 MINS

2 ½ cups finely chopped broccoli florets

10 large eggs

½ cup cooked yellow lentils

⅔ cup grated sharp Cheddar cheese

⅓ cup diced roasted red peppers

Pinch paprika

Salt and pepper

1 Preheat the oven to 350°F (180°C). Heat a skillet over medium-low heat. Add broccoli and cook for 2 to 3 minutes until bright green but still crisp. Remove from heat and let cool slightly.

2 In a large mixing bowl, whisk eggs. Add broccoli, lentils, Cheddar, red peppers, and paprika. Season with salt and pepper.

3 With cooking spray, heavily coat each cup of a 12-cup muffin pan. Portion egg mixture evenly into each cup.

4 Bake for 20 minutes, or until completely set. Run a butter knife around each muffin to help release from the pan. Serve immediately or let cool completely and store in an airtight container in the refrigerator for up to 2 days.

Nutrition per muffin	
Calories	100
Total Fat	6g
Saturated Fat	2.5g
Cholesterol	160mg
Sodium	310mg
Total Carbohydrate	3g
Dietary Fiber	1g
Sugars	<1g
Protein	8g

● **Make it with meat**

Add ⅓ cup cooked and diced ham or bacon to egg mixture before baking.

BLACK BEAN COCOA SMOOTHIE

Black beans and chocolate are an unusual match in this smoothie, which is both a sweet treat and a healthful start to your day.

MAKES 2 · PREP 10 MINS

1 cup milk

½ cup cooked black beans

1 large ripe banana

3 tbsp unsweetened cocoa powder

1 tbsp agave nectar

½ cup crushed ice cubes

1 In a blender, add milk and black beans. Blend until smooth.

2 Add banana, cocoa powder, agave, and crushed ice. Blend once more until smooth. Pour smoothie into 2 glasses and serve immediately.

Nutrition per smoothie	
Calories	240
Total Fat	4g
Saturated Fat	1g
Cholesterol	0mg
Sodium	55mg
Total Carbohydrate	45g
Dietary Fiber	8g
Sugars	21g
Protein	12g

● **Make it vegan**

Replace milk with an equal amount unsweetened soy or almond milk.

SPICED APPLE & MUNG BEAN MUFFINS

Mung beans puréed with applesauce make for one of the moistest muffins you'll ever taste and add protein and fiber for a filling on-the-go breakfast.

MAKES 12 · PREP 35 MINS · COOK 20 MINS

⅔ cup unsweetened applesauce

½ cup cooked mung beans

2 tbsp agave nectar

¾ cup whole-wheat flour

¾ cup all-purpose flour

2 tsp baking powder

1 tsp cinnamon

Pinch ground nutmeg

1 large egg

½ cup packed light brown sugar

⅓ cup unsweetened almond milk

1 medium Granny Smith apple, peeled, cored, and finely diced (about 1 cup)

¼ cup rolled oats

1 Preheat the oven to 350°F (175°C). In a food processor, combine applesauce, mung beans, and agave. Purée until smooth.

2 In a large mixing bowl, whisk together whole-wheat flour, all-purpose flour, baking powder, cinnamon, and nutmeg.

3 In a medium mixing bowl, add egg, brown sugar, almond milk, and applesauce-mung bean mixture. Whisk to combine thoroughly.

4 Add egg–mung bean mixture to flour mixture bowl and stir just until no streaks of dry ingredients remain. Gently fold in diced apples until just combined.

5 Line a 12-cup muffin pan with paper liners. Portion 2 tablespoons batter into each cup. Sprinkle top of each muffin with 1 teaspoon oats. Bake for 20 to 25 minutes until set and a toothpick inserted into center of muffin comes out clean. Let rest for an hour before serving. Store in an airtight container for up to 2 days.

Nutrition per muffin

Calories	110
Total Fat	0.5g
Saturated Fat	0g
Cholesterol	0mg
Sodium	5mg
Total Carbohydrate	25g
Dietary Fiber	2g
Sugars	10g
Protein	2g

● Make it vegan

Substitute ¼ cup mashed banana instead of egg.

for free! Visit indigo.ca/plumrewards to learn more.

Chapters   !ndigo   COLES   indigo.ca

Refunds or exchanges may be made within 14 days if item is returned in
pre-bought condition with a receipt. Items with a gift receipt may be exchanged
or refunded onto a credit note for the value of the item at the time of purchase.
We cannot provide an exchange or refund on magazines or newspapers.

plum™ rewards

Points Required	Reward Value
2,500	$5
4,500	$10
8,500	$20
20,000	$50
35,000	$100

Explore the benefits of plum rewards and become a member
for free! Visit indigo.ca/plumrewards to learn more.

Chapters   !ndigo   COLES   indigo.ca

Refunds or exchanges may be made within 14 days if item is returned in
re-bought condition with a receipt. Items with a gift receipt may be exchanged
refunded onto a credit note for the value of the item at the time of purchase.
We cannot provide an exchange or refund on magazines or newspapers.

plum™ rewards

Points Required	Reward Value
2,500	$5
4,500	$10

YELLOW LENTIL WAFFLES
WITH FIVE SPICE BERRY SAUCE

Crispy on the outside, yet soft and light on the inside, these wholesome waffles are mild and slightly nutty. The five spice powder in the berry sauce makes the sweetness of the berries sing.

MAKES 4 · PREP 15 MINS · COOK 15 MINS

6oz (170g) fresh raspberries

6oz (170g) fresh blackberries

6oz (170g) fresh blueberries

¼ tsp five spice powder

1 cinnamon stick

3 tbsp water

1 ¼ cups unsweetened almond milk

¼ cup canola oil

2 tsp vanilla extract

3 tbsp agave nectar

1 ½ cups whole-wheat flour

1 ½ tsp baking powder

½ cup cooked yellow lentils

1 In a small saucepan, combine raspberries, blackberries, blueberries, five spice powder, and cinnamon stick. Cook, covered, over low heat for 15 minutes, or until berries break down into a thickened sauce, stirring regularly. Add 2 to 3 tablespoons water as needed.

2 Meanwhile, in a small bowl, whisk together almond milk, oil, vanilla, and agave.

3 Preheat a waffle maker. In a large mixing bowl, combine whole-wheat flour and baking powder. Incorporate almond milk mixture into flour mixture. Gently fold in lentils.

4 Once heated, spray each section of the waffle iron with cooking spray. Portion ½ cup batter into each section of the waffle maker. Cook according to the manufacturer's instructions to make 4 waffles total.

5 Remove cinnamon stick from berry sauce. Serve waffles immediately with sauce.

Nutrition per waffle

Calories	350
Total Fat	10g
Saturated Fat	0.5g
Cholesterol	0mg
Sodium	80mg
Total Carbohydrate	50g
Dietary Fiber	13g
Sugars	6g
Protein	13g

Pulse exchange
Use an equal amount **red lentils** instead of yellow lentils.

MOTH BEAN GREEN SMOOTHIE

Adding moth beans to your green smoothie is a simple way to fortify your morning drink with even more protein and fiber.

MAKES 2 · PREP 10 MINS

⅔ cup unsweetened almond milk or soy milk

1 ½ cups diced fresh pineapple

2 cups baby spinach

⅓ cup cooked moth beans

1 ripe banana

⅓ cup crushed ice cubes

1 In a blender, pour in almond milk then add pineapple, spinach, moth beans, and banana. Blend until smooth.

2 Add crushed ice and blend once more until smooth. Pour smoothie into 2 glasses and serve immediately.

Nutrition per smoothie

Calories	160	Sodium	85mg
Total Fat	1.5g	Total Carbohydrate	37g
Saturated Fat	0g	Dietary Fiber	6g
Cholesterol	0mg	Sugars	19g
		Protein	5g

LEMON POPPY SEED PANCAKES

Poppy seeds add unexpected texture to these fluffy, flavorful pancakes.

MAKES 4 · PREP 30 MINS · COOK 20 MINS

¾ cup unsweetened almond milk

3 tbsp lemon juice

Zest 2 lemons

2 tbsp fluid coconut oil

1 tsp vanilla extract

2 ½ tbsp granulated sugar

1 tsp baking soda

1 tsp baking powder

1 cup chickpea flour

1 tbsp poppy seeds

1 In a small mixing bowl, combine almond milk, lemon juice, lemon zest, coconut oil, vanilla, and sugar.

2 In a large mixing bowl, whisk together baking soda, baking powder, chickpea flour, and poppy seeds. Pour almond milk mixture into flour mixture and gently stir just until smooth. Gently fold in poppy seeds until combined. Let batter rest for 10 minutes without stirring.

3 Heat a medium nonstick skillet or griddle over medium heat. Portion out a quarter of batter and pour into the skillet. Cook for 2 minutes, or until bubbles form along outer edge and throughout middle. Gently flip and cook for an additional 1 to 2 minutes. Remove from heat and repeat with remaining batter to make 4 pancakes total. Serve immediately with butter or maple syrup.

Nutrition per pancake

Calories	140	Sodium	240mg
Total Fat	7g	Total Carbohydrate	16g
Saturated Fat	4g	Dietary Fiber	2g
Cholesterol	0mg	Sugars	6g
		Protein	4g

BEAN & QUINOA BREAKFAST BOWLS

Kidney beans simmered with herbs and spices create a deeply flavorful base for these hearty, satisfying breakfast bowls.

SERVES 8 · PREP 15 MINS · COOK 1 HR 30 MINS

1 tbsp vegetable oil

1 medium yellow onion, chopped

1 green bell pepper, deseeded and chopped

2 celery stalks, diced

2 garlic cloves, minced

2 bay leaves

4 thyme sprigs

3 cups soaked kidney beans

8 cups vegetable stock

¾ tsp ground cayenne pepper

¾ tsp smoked paprika

Salt and pepper

1 cup dry quinoa

1 large avocado, sliced

1 cup cilantro leaves

Hot sauce, optional

1 In a large Dutch oven or stockpot, heat oil over medium-low heat until shimmering. Add onion, bell pepper, and celery. Cook for 2 to 3 minutes until soft. Add garlic and cook for an additional 1 to 2 minutes.

2 Add bay leaves, thyme, and soaked kidney beans. Stir in 6 cups stock, cayenne, and paprika. Bring to a boil then reduce heat and simmer, covered, for 60 to 75 minutes until beans are tender, stirring occasionally. Season with salt and pepper to taste.

3 Meanwhile, in a separate pot, bring remaining 2 cups stock to a boil over medium heat. Stir in quinoa and return to a boil. Reduce the heat to low and cook, covered, for 20 minutes, or until all stock is absorbed. Remove from the heat and let sit, covered.

4 Remove bay leaf and thyme stems from bean mixture. To serve, use a slotted spoon and portion quinoa into bowls. Top with bean mixture, adding cooking liquid as desired. Garnish with avocado and cilantro. Serve immediately, with hot sauce, if using.

● Make it with meat

For a smoky element, add ¼ cup raw, chopped, thick-cut bacon and cook along with onions.

Nutrition per serving

Calories	400
Total Fat	8g
Saturated Fat	2g
Cholesterol	0mg
Sodium	160mg
Total Carbohydrate	65g
Dietary Fiber	16g
Sugars	6g
Protein	20g

Why not try... For added richness, top each bowl with a fried egg—yolk makes an excellent sauce for beans and quinoa.

TROPICAL SMOOTHIE BOWL

The bright flavors of pineapple and mango are complemented by velvety white beans and banana in these beautiful, protein-rich bowls.

● Make it vegan

Use a vegan yogurt alternative rather than vanilla yogurt.

MAKES 2 · PREP 10 MINS

1 cup diced mango

1 cup diced pineapple

1 banana, sliced

1 tbsp honey or agave nectar

¾ cup low-fat vanilla yogurt

½ cup cooked Great Northern beans

¼ cup toasted coconut, to garnish

2 tsp chia seeds, to garnish

1 Withhold a bit of mango, pineapple, and banana for garnish. In a blender, add remainder of fruit along with honey, yogurt, and Great Northern beans. Purée until completely smooth.

2 Divide smoothie between two bowls, and garnish with toasted coconut, chia seeds, and reserved mango, pineapple, and banana. Serve immediately.

Pulse exchange

Substitute an equal amount **navy beans** rather than Great Northern beans.

Nutrition per bowl

Calories	370
Total Fat	7g
Saturated Fat	4.5g
Cholesterol	<5mg
Sodium	95mg
Total Carbohydrate	72g
Dietary Fiber	9g
Sugars	51g
Protein	9g

SNACKS
& SPREADS

MUNG BEAN GUACAMOLE

The addition of mung beans brings a nutritional boost and an extra creamy texture to this Mexican classic. Serve with tortilla chips or alongside your favorite tacos.

SERVES 2 · PREP 20 MINS

2 large avocados

Juice 1 lime

1 white onion, finely chopped

2 garlic cloves, minced

1 medium tomato, diced

½ cup cooked mung beans

2 tbsp roughly chopped cilantro

Salt and pepper

1 Cut avocados in half, remove pits, and scoop flesh into a large bowl. Immediately add lime juice. With a pastry cutter or fork, roughly mash avocado.

2 Add onion, garlic, tomato, mung beans, and cilantro. Gently stir to combine. Season with salt and pepper to taste. Serve immediately.

Pulse exchange
You can replace mung beans with an equal amount **Great Northern** or **navy beans.**

Nutrition per serving

Calories	300
Total Fat	21g
Saturated Fat	3g
Cholesterol	0mg
Sodium	170mg
Total Carbohydrate	25g
Dietary Fiber	15g
Sugars	4g
Protein	7g

YELLOW LENTIL DEVILED EGGS

Basil, oregano, and lemon juice brighten these deviled eggs, a picnic and party favorite. Incorporating yellow lentils into the filling adds texture and updates the classic recipe.

MAKES 12 · PREP 20 MINS · COOK 10 MINS

6 large eggs
⅓ cup cooked yellow lentils
¼ cup mayonnaise or sour cream
¾ tsp Dijon mustard
¼ cup chopped basil
¼ cup chopped oregano
½ tbsp lemon juice
Salt and pepper
Chopped chervil or chopped chives, to garnish

1 Bring a large pot of water to a rolling boil and carefully lower eggs into water. Boil for 9 minutes, then immediately remove and place in an ice bath to cool completely.

2 Peel off shells and slice eggs in half lengthwise. Scoop out and reserve yolks. Reserve whites to fill.

3 To make filling, in a food processor add yolks, lentils, mayonnaise, mustard, basil, and oregano. Process on low, slowly drizzling in lemon juice. Purée until smooth. Taste and season with salt and pepper.

4 Carefully spoon or pipe about 1 tablespoon filling into each egg half. Garnish with chervil or chives. Serve immediately or store in an airtight container in the refrigerator for up to 2 days.

Nutrition per deviled egg

Calories	80
Total Fat	6g
Saturated Fat	1.5g
Cholesterol	95mg
Sodium	160mg
Total Carbohydrate	3g
Dietary Fiber	1g
Sugars	0g
Protein	4g

● **Make it with meat**

Garnish deviled eggs with 2 tablespoons orange tobiko or another colorful caviar.

ADZUKI BEAN SUMMER ROLLS
WITH PEANUT SAUCE

Spiralized jicama replaces traditional rice noodles in these summer rolls. Adzuki beans work well with the sweetness of the mango and the creaminess of the avocado.

MAKES 16 · PREP 1 HR

½ cup creamy peanut butter

Juice 1 lime

1 tbsp rice wine vinegar

⅓ cup water

½ tsp Sriracha

1 small jicama, peeled

1oz (25g) mint leaves

1 mango, peeled, pitted, and cut into ½-in (1cm) slices

1 small red onion, julienned

1 avocado, pitted and cut into ¼-in (½cm) slices

1 ½ cups cooked adzuki beans

2 cups cilantro leaves

12oz (340g) pkg spring roll rice paper wrappers

1 To make peanut sauce, in a small bowl whisk together peanut butter, lime juice, vinegar, water, and Sriracha until smooth. Set aside until ready to serve.

2 Cut jicama into even chunks. Adjust a spiralizer to the thinnest blade and spiralize jicama. Prepare your workspace with jicama, mint, mango, onion, avocado, adzuki beans, and cilantro to fill rolls.

3 Pour warm water into a shallow pie pan. Working one at a time, submerge rice paper wrapper into warm water for 30 seconds, or until pliable without tearing. Remove from water and place onto a clean, flat surface on which the wrapper will not stick (like a plastic or ceramic cutting board).

4 Arrange the desired amount mint leaves, mango, red onion, avocado, adzuki beans, cilantro, and spiralized jicama in center of wrapper, being sure to work quickly so the wrapper doesn't dry. Do not over-stuff ingredients, or wrapper will tear. Fold bottom edge of wrapper over filling, and press to seal. Then fold sides of wrapper toward center, tucking in filling. Gently roll and firmly seal.

5 Repeat to use all remaining ingredients. Serve with peanut sauce on the side. So they do not stick together, store individually wrapped in the refrigerator for 2 to 3 days.

● **Make it with meat**

Horizontally slice 1 cooked shrimp and place atop mint during assembly of each roll.

Nutrition per summer roll

Calories	178
Total Fat	6g
Saturated Fat	1g
Cholesterol	0mg
Sodium	40mg
Total Carbohydrate	25g
Dietary Fiber	4g
Sugars	1g
Protein	4g

LEMONY SPINACH HUMMUS

The bold green color of this citrusy hummus screams healthy. The fresh garnishes and bright flavor taste great with pita bread or as a spread for wraps and sandwiches.

SERVES 6 · PREP 5 MINS · COOK 5 MINS

1 cup cooked chickpeas, peeled

4 cups baby spinach

2 garlic cloves

Juice and zest 1 large lemon

1 tbsp tahini

¼ cup olive oil

Salt and pepper

1 ½ tbsp chia seeds, to garnish

Alfalfa sprouts, to garnish

Microgreens, to garnish

1 In a food processor, combine chickpeas, spinach, garlic, lemon juice and zest, and tahini. Process on low for 1 minute to combine ingredients.

2 With the processor on high, drizzle in oil. For a thinner consistency, gradually add cold water, 1 tablespoon at a time until desired texture is achieved.

3 Transfer to a serving bowl and garnish with chia seeds, sprouts, and microgreens. Serve immediately.

● **Make it with meat**

For a Middle Eastern appetizer, top with 8oz (250g) sautéed, ground lamb, spiced as desired.

Nutrition per serving

Calories	140
Total Fat	10g
Saturated Fat	1.5g
Cholesterol	0mg
Sodium	20mg
Total Carbohydrate	11g
Dietary Fiber	4g
Sugars	2g
Protein	4g

Pulse exchange

Substitute an equal amount **Great Northern** or **navy beans** rather than chickpeas.

BELUGA LENTIL & OLIVE TAPENADE

This olive spread from the Provence region of France is a flavorful make-ahead appetizer. Serve with a toasted baguette or crudités.

SERVES 6 · PREP 5 MINS · COOK 5 MINS

1 cup Kalamata olives, pitted
1 cup cooked beluga lentils
2 garlic cloves
1 ½ tbsp drained capers
¼ cup olive oil

1 In a food processor, add olives, lentils, garlic, and capers. Pulse to combine.

2 With the processor running on low, drizzle in oil until smooth and fully combined. Serve immediately or store in an airtight container in the refrigerator for up to 3 days.

BLACK-EYED PEA HUMMUS

This dip has a light, whipped texture that pairs well with cucumber slices and radishes or toasted pita bread.

SERVES 6 · PREP 15 MINS

2 cups plus 2 tbsp cooked black-eyed peas
3 tbsp tahini
1 garlic clove
Juice 1 lemon
¼ tsp smoked paprika
¼ cup olive oil
Salt and pepper

1 In a food processor, combine black-eyed peas, tahini, garlic, lemon juice, and paprika. Pulse to incorporate.

2 With the processor running on low, drizzle in oil until smooth. For a thinner consistency, add up to ¼ cup water and blend until smooth. Taste and season with salt and pepper and pulse once more to incorporate.

3 Transfer to a serving bowl and garnish with remaining 2 tablespoons black-eyed peas and dash smoked paprika. Serve immediately or store in an airtight container in the refrigerator for up to 2 days.

Nutrition per serving

Calories	220
Total Fat	12g
Saturated Fat	1.5g
Cholesterol	0mg
Sodium	105mg
Total Carbohydrate	23g
Dietary Fiber	6g
Sugars	<1g
Protein	8g

●Make it with meat

For an extra briny punch, add to mixture 2 anchovy fillets from a 2-ounce (55g) can.

Nutrition per serving

Calories	170
Total Fat	11g
Saturated Fat	1.5g
Cholesterol	0mg
Sodium	105mg
Total Carbohydrate	14g
Dietary Fiber	3g
Sugars	<1g
Protein	6g

CHICKPEA FRIES

For a satisfying, salty snack, the fried chickpea batter in this recipe creates fries with a thin, crispy exterior that contrasts a lightly spiced, silky interior.

● **Make it with meat**

For greater depth of flavor, use chicken stock rather than vegetable stock.

SERVES 6 · PREP 5 MINS, PLUS 2 HRS TO CHILL · COOK 10 MINS

1 cup chickpea flour

2 cups vegetable stock

¼ tsp garam masala

Dash cinnamon

2 cups vegetable oil or canola oil

Salt and pepper

1 Spray an 8x8-inch (20x20cm) glass baking dish lightly with cooking spray. Set aside.

2 In a saucepan, combine chickpea flour, stock, garam masala, and cinnamon over medium-low heat. Bring to a boil then reduce to a simmer. Cook, covered, for 8 to 9 minutes, whisking constantly until batter thickens to the consistency of creamy peanut butter.

3 Remove from heat. Transfer batter to the prepared baking dish and spread evenly. Cover with aluminum foil or plastic wrap and refrigerate for 2 hours or overnight until completely set.

4 Turn the dish upside down to release batter onto a clean, flat work surface. Blot both sides with a paper towel to remove excess moisture. Cut square in half, then cut each half into 12 to 14 thin rectangles to make 24 to 28 fries.

5 Line a baking sheet with paper towel. In a heavy-bottomed 8 ½-inch (22cm) skillet, heat oil over medium heat. When oil is hot and shimmering, add chickpea fries in batches so they lay in an even layer. Cook for 2 to 3 minutes on each side until golden brown. Transfer to the baking sheet to absorb excess oil. Repeat to cook remaining fries. Season with salt and pepper and serve immediately.

Nutrition per serving

Calories	220
Total Fat	19g
Saturated Fat	15g
Cholesterol	0mg
Sodium	55mg
Total Carbohydrate	10g
Dietary Fiber	2g
Sugars	2g
Protein	3g

Why not try... For an unusual treat, dust these fries with powdered sugar to give them a sweet and salty contrast.

SPICY CARROT HUMMUS

Harissa is a natural match for the sweetness of carrots and the tang of tahini in this hummus. Serve with crisp vegetables or seeded crackers.

SERVES 6 · PREP 20 MINS · COOK 30 MINS

¾ lb (340g) carrots, ends trimmed (7-8 carrots)

¼ cup plus 1 tbsp olive oil

2 cups cooked chickpeas, peeled

1 tbsp water

1 ½ tbsp tahini

Juice 1 large lime

1 tbsp harissa paste

Salt and pepper

1 Preheat the oven to 350°F (180°C). Peel carrots and cut into 1-inch (3cm) chunks. Toss with 1 tablespoon oil and arrange in a single layer on a baking sheet. Roast for 25 to 30 minutes until caramelized and tender. Remove from oven and let cool.

2 In a food processor, combine chickpeas with water and whir briefly to combine. Add tahini, lime juice, harissa, and roasted carrots. With the processor running on low, drizzle in remaining ¼ cup oil. Taste and season with salt and pepper, then pulse a few more times to combine. Serve immediately.

Pulse exchange
Replace chickpeas with an equal amount cooked **Great Northern** or **navy beans.**

Nutrition per serving

Calories	240
Total Fat	16g
Saturated Fat	2g
Cholesterol	0mg
Sodium	250mg
Total Carbohydrate	22g
Dietary Fiber	6g
Sugars	6g
Protein	6g

WHITE BEAN BUTTER
WITH RADISHES

Radishes with butter and salt are a classic French snack. Here, the butter is browned and blended with white beans to make a luxurious and creamy dip.

SERVES 4 · PREP 5 MINS · COOK 10 MINS

2 tbsp unsalted butter

1 cup cooked Great Northern beans

1 garlic clove

1 tsp water (optional)

1 bunch radishes, washed and tops removed

Flaky sea salt

1 In a small saucepan, melt butter over low heat. Cook until butter takes on a light brown color and nutty aroma, then remove from heat.

2 In a food processor, combine butter, Great Northern beans, and garlic. Blend on high until smooth, adding water as needed to reach the desired consistency.

3 Transfer white bean dip to a small bowl and serve alongside radishes and a small dish of sea salt.

Nutrition per serving

Calories	110
Total Fat	6g
Saturated Fat	3.5g
Cholesterol	15mg
Sodium	10mg
Total Carbohydrate	10g
Dietary Fiber	3g
Sugars	<1g
Protein	4g

● **Make it vegan**

Omit butter and you will have a more traditional white bean dip.

SPIRALIZED BEET & ONION BHAJIS
WITH CUCUMBER SAUCE

These crispy Indian fritters are eaten as an appetizer or snack. The spiralized beets in this version add a vivid pink color.

MAKES 12 · PREP 15 MINS · COOK 15 MINS

1 quart canola oil

1 cup plain Greek yogurt

1 small cucumber, peeled and grated

1 large yellow onion, peeled

1 large beet, peeled

Dash turmeric

½ tsp salt

¾ cup chickpea flour

½ cup water

1 In a large Dutch oven or heavy-bottomed pot, heat canola oil over medium-low heat. Measuring with a deep frying thermometer, bring to 350°F (180°C).

2 Meanwhile, to make cucumber sauce, in a small bowl stir together Greek yogurt and cucumber.

3 Adjust a spiralizer to the thinnest blade and spiralize onion and beet. With kitchen shears, trim into 1-inch (3cm) lengths.

4 In a large mixing bowl, whisk together turmeric, salt, chickpea flour, and water. Gradually add water until batter is the consistency of pancake batter. Add beet and onion and toss to combine.

5 With your hands, gather 2 tablespoons bhaji mixture and carefully drop into oil. Fry for 4 minutes, or until golden and crispy, rotating once. Place on a plate lined with paper towel and repeat with remaining batter. Serve immediately with cucumber sauce.

Nutrition per bhaji

Calories	210
Total Fat	19g
Saturated Fat	1.5g
Cholesterol	0mg
Sodium	110mg
Total Carbohydrate	7g
Dietary Fiber	1g
Sugars	3g
Protein	4g

● Make it vegan

Replace Greek yogurt in dipping sauce with an equal amount coconut milk yogurt.

NAVY BEAN & ARTICHOKE PAN BAGNAT

This French sandwich is the ultimate picnic or packed lunch recipe. It gets better the longer it sits as the bread absorbs the vinaigrette and vegetable flavor.

MAKES 4 · PREP 50 MINS

3 tbsp red wine vinegar

1 ½ tbsp olive oil

1 small cucumber, peeled, deseeded, and thinly sliced

1 small red onion, thinly sliced

14oz (396g) can artichoke hearts, drained

1 cup cooked navy beans

2 garlic cloves

½ cup drained cornichons

¼ cup flat-leaf parsley leaves

2 tbsp plain Greek yogurt

Pinch red pepper flakes

Salt and pepper

1 whole-wheat baguette

12 large basil leaves

1 Roma tomato, thinly sliced

2 hard-boiled eggs, peeled and thinly sliced

⅓ cup pitted Niçoise olives, roughly chopped

Nutrition per sandwich

Calories	320
Total Fat	6g
Saturated Fat	1g
Cholesterol	0mg
Sodium	920mg
Total Carbohydrate	52g
Dietary Fiber	11g
Sugars	6g
Protein	13g

1 In a medium mixing bowl, combine red wine vinegar, oil, cucumber, and red onion. Toss to combine and set aside. Let marinate while you prepare the rest of sandwich.

2 In a food processor, combine artichoke hearts, navy beans, garlic, cornichons, parsley, yogurt, and red pepper flakes. Pulse until combined but not smooth. Taste and season with salt and pepper.

3 Slice baguette in half lengthwise to make a long sub. Lay the two halves cut-side up on the work surface. To make space for ingredients, remove about a 1-inch (3cm) wide channel of bread from each side.

4 To assemble sandwich, in the bottom half of baguette arrange basil leaves in a single layer. Top with artichoke–navy bean mixture in an even layer. Then top with Roma tomato and hard-boiled egg.

5 In the top of baguette, evenly spread cucumber and red onion mixture. Drizzle on any remaining liquid. Top with Niçoise olives.

6 Carefully place the top half of baguette atop the bottom half. Slice into 4 equal sandwiches. Wrap each with parchment paper and let marinate in the refrigerator for at least 30 minutes or overnight.

Make it vegan
Omit egg and use dairy-free yogurt substitute rather than Greek yogurt.

Make it with meat
For more briny flavor, add 8 canned anchovy filets along with olives.

SUMAC ROASTED CHICKPEAS

Salty, tangy, and crispy, these roasted chickpeas are a healthy and addictive snack.

SERVES 4 · PREP 5 MINS · COOK 1 HR

2 tbsp olive oil
Zest and juice 2 lemons
2 tsp sumac

1 tsp kosher salt
4 cups cooked chickpeas, thoroughly drained and dried

1 Preheat the oven to 375°F (190°C). In a large mixing bowl, combine oil, lemon zest and juice, sumac, and salt. Add chickpeas and toss to coat thoroughly. Spread chickpeas in an even layer on a baking sheet.

2 Bake for 40 to 45 minutes until golden brown and lightly crisp, stirring every 10 to 15 minutes. Remove the baking sheet from the oven and place on a wire cooling rack. Let cool completely on the tray. Serve immediately or store in an airtight container for up to 3 days.

CHICKPEA ENERGY BITES

These peanut butter energy bites are a wonderful make-ahead snack for lunches or a mid-day treat.

MAKES 24 · PREP 20 MINS, PLUS 1 HR TO SET

2 cups cooked chickpeas
½ cup creamy peanut butter
½ cup rolled oats

⅓ cup agave nectar
1 tsp vanilla extract
1 tsp cinnamon
Pinch salt

1 In a food processor, pulse chickpeas until coarsely ground. Transfer to a large mixing bowl. Stir in peanut butter, oats, agave, vanilla, cinnamon, and salt.

2 Portion out a heaping tablespoon chickpea mixture and roll into a ball with your hands. Repeat with remaining chickpea mixture to make 24 total. Refrigerate in an airtight container for at least 1 hour or overnight to set before serving.

Nutrition per serving

Calories	330	Sodium	570mg
Total Fat	11g	Total Carbohydrate	47g
Saturated Fat	1.5g	Dietary Fiber	13g
		Sugars	8g
Cholesterol	0mg	Protein	15g

Nutrition per bite

Calories	70	Sodium	45mg
Total Fat	3g	Total Carbohydrate	10g
Saturated Fat	0g	Dietary Fiber	2g
		Sugars	5g
Cholesterol	0mg	Protein	3g

QUINOA & MOTH BEAN DOLMADES

The distinct flavors of dill and mint combine with the textures of currants and pine nuts in these stuffed grape leaves, whose flavors strengthen with time for a delicious make-ahead lunch.

MAKES 24 · PREP 30 MINS · COOK 1 HR

8oz (227g) jar whole grape leaves

1 cup cooked quinoa

1 ½ tbsp chopped mint

1 ½ tbsp chopped dill

1 ½ tbsp chopped flat-leaf parsley

¼ cup dried currants

¼ cup toasted pine nuts

2 tbsp olive oil

3 tbsp lemon juice

Salt and pepper

1 cup cooked moth beans

1 cup vegetable stock

1 Preheat the oven to 350°F (180°C). Lightly coat a 9x13-inch (23x33cm) glass or ceramic baking dish with cooking spray. Fill a large bowl with warm water. Soak grape leaves for 2 to 3 minutes until pliable. Drain into a colander. Cover the colander with a wet towel so they remain moist during assembly.

2 To make filling, in a large mixing bowl combine quinoa, mint, dill, parsley, currants, pine nuts, 1 tablespoon oil, 1 tablespoon lemon juice, and cooked moth beans. Season with salt and pepper.

3 To assemble dolmades, place one grape leaf on a clean, flat work surface, vein-side up, and cut off stem. Add 1 heaping tablespoon filling in center, toward bottom of leaf. Fold sides of leaf over filling and roll from stem-end to tip to make a tight roll. Place seam-side down in the baking dish. Repeat with remaining leaves, arranging snugly together.

4 Pour stock over dolmades and drizzle on remaining 1 tablespoon oil and remaining 2 tablespoons lemon juice.

5 Cover the baking dish with aluminum foil and bake for 20 to 30 minutes until all liquid absorbs and dolmades are moist and steaming. Serve immediately or let cool and store in the refrigerator in an airtight container for up to 2 days.

● **Make it with meat**

Stir in 1 ½ ounces (40g) cooked ground lamb or beef with quinoa filling.

Why not try...

For a brinier bite, sprinkle ⅓ cup finely crumbled feta cheese into quinoa filling before rolling dolmades.

Nutrition per dolma

Calories	60
Total Fat	2.5g
Saturated Fat	0g
Cholesterol	0mg
Sodium	220mg
Total Carbohydrate	7g
Dietary Fiber	2g
Sugars	2g
Protein	2g

MASALA CHICKPEA NACHOS

This hybrid recipe combines the warm spices of Indian cuisine with the comfort and crunchiness of traditional Mexican nachos.

SERVES 6 · PREP 40 MINS · COOK 20 MINS

3 cups packed cilantro leaves

1 cup mint leaves

2 tbsp lemon juice

¼ tsp ground ginger

⅓ cup plus 1 tbsp cold water

Salt and pepper

2 cups cooked chickpeas

1 tsp curry powder

1 tsp garam masala

1 tbsp vegetable oil

10 papadum, cooked according to pkg instructions

2 cups shredded mozzarella cheese

½ cup mango chutney

¼ cup diced red onion

1 large lime, cut into 6 wedges

1 To make cilantro-mint sauce, in a blender combine 2 cups cilantro, mint, lemon juice, ginger, and ⅓ cup water. Purée until smooth. Season with salt and pepper. Transfer to an airtight container and set aside.

2 Preheat the oven to 400°F (200°C). Line a rimmed baking sheet with foil. Toss chickpeas with curry powder, garam masala, and oil. Spread in an even layer on the baking sheet and bake for 10 minutes, or until slightly crispy and warmed through. Transfer chickpeas to a bowl and wipe off the baking sheet.

3 Break each papadum into quarters and arrange in a single layer on the baking sheet. Sprinkle half of mozzarella over papadum and top with chickpea mixture. Then top with remaining mozzarella and bake for 10 to 12 minutes until mozzarella melts and papadum are lightly brown.

4 Meanwhile, in a small saucepan, heat mango chutney with remaining 1 tablespoon water. Cook for 2 to 3 minutes until thin and warmed through.

5 To finish assembly, sprinkle onion over melted cheese. Drizzle mango chutney sauce over the top. Dollop cilantro-mint sauce across nachos. Chop remaining 1 cup cilantro and sprinkle over nachos. Garnish with lime wedges and serve immediately, directly from the sheet.

Make it vegan

Use a soy mozzarella cheese alternative instead of regular mozzarella.

Make it with meat

Layer 4 ½ ounces (130g) cooked, shredded chicken with chickpeas in step 3.

Nutrition per serving

Calories	420
Total Fat	18g
Saturated Fat	12g
Cholesterol	40mg
Sodium	660mg
Total Carbohydrate	40g
Dietary Fiber	6g
Sugars	13g
Protein	26g

EVERYTHING CHICKPEA FLOUR CRACKERS

Chickpea flour has a nutty flavor that pairs well with these everything bagel-inspired crackers. The crunchy seeds enhance the texture and go well with your favorite hummus or dip.

MAKES 24 · PREP 30 MINS · COOK 15 MINS

½ tbsp sesame seeds

½ tbsp black sesame seeds

½ tbsp poppy seeds

½ tsp baking powder

1 cup chickpea flour

¾ tsp salt

⅛ tsp onion powder

⅛ tsp garlic powder

2 tbsp olive oil

⅓ cup water

1 To make topping, in a small bowl mix together sesame seeds, black sesame seeds, and poppy seeds. Set aside.

2 Preheat the oven to 375°F (190°C). Prepare a clean, flat work area and cut two large pieces of parchment paper of equal size, about 12x16-inches (31x41cm).

3 To make dough, in a large mixing bowl combine baking powder, chickpea flour, salt, onion powder, garlic powder, and oil. Gradually incorporate ¼ cup water until dough forms, adding additional water a spoonful at a time as needed, just until dough is pliable. Place in the refrigerator and let rest for 10 minutes.

4 Divide dough into two pieces and place side-by-side between the two sheets of parchment paper, about 5 inches (13cm) apart. With a rolling pin, roll out as thinly as possible into 2 rectangles, about ⅛ inch (3mm) thick.

5 Remove the top sheet of parchment paper. With a pizza cutter or paring knife, score rolled dough into 1x1-inch (3x3cm) squares for 24 total crackers. Brush dough with 1 to 2 teaspoons water, then sprinkle seed mixture evenly across the top.

6 Transfer the bottom piece of parchment paper directly onto a rimless baking sheet. Bake for 10 to 15 minutes until edges start to brown and crackers are firm. Let rest at room temperature for 5 minutes then break crackers apart. Store in an airtight container for up to 3 days.

Nutrition per cracker

Calories	30
Total Fat	1.5g
Saturated Fat	0g
Cholesterol	0mg
Sodium	75mg
Total Carbohydrate	2g
Dietary Fiber	0g
Sugars	0g
Protein	1g

RED LENTIL CAPONATA

Caponata is a sweet-and-sour Sicilian eggplant dish often served as a dip or appetizer.

SERVES 6 · PREP 25 MINS · COOK 1 HR

1 large eggplant, cubed

3 tbsp olive oil

1 medium yellow onion, diced

2 garlic cloves, minced

1 celery stalk, chopped

2 large tomatoes, deseeded and chopped

3 tbsp capers

2 tbsp toasted pine nuts

¼ cup golden raisins

½ cup cooked red lentils

1 tbsp granulated sugar

⅓ cup red wine vinegar

Pinch red pepper flakes

Dash cinnamon

Dash unsweetened cocoa powder

Salt and pepper

1 Preheat the oven to 400°F (200°C). Spread eggplant on a baking sheet. Drizzle with 2 tablespoons oil. Roast for 20 minutes, or until tender.

2 In a large skillet, heat remaining 1 tablespoon oil. Add onion and cook for 2 to 3 minutes until soft. Add garlic and cook for 1 minute. Add celery, tomatoes, and eggplant. Cook for 5 minutes.

3 Add capers, pine nuts, raisins, lentils, sugar, vinegar, red pepper flakes, cinnamon, and cocoa powder. Simmer for 10 minutes, covered. Taste and season with salt and pepper. Remove from heat and let cool. Refrigerate in an airtight container for 2 hours or overnight before serving.

Nutrition per serving

Calories	180	Sodium	500mg
Total Fat	11g	Total Carbohydrate	22g
Saturated Fat	1.5g	Dietary Fiber	6g
Cholesterol	0mg	Sugars	12g
		Protein	4g

RED PEPPER & WHITE BEAN DIP

This flavor-packed, 15-minute dip is the ultimate recipe for easy entertaining.

SERVES 8 · PREP 15 MINS

2 cups cooked chickpeas

1 ½ cups roasted red peppers, drained

2 cups cooked Great Northern beans

Zest and juice 1 lemon

1 tsp red pepper flakes

1 tbsp thyme leaves

1 tbsp chopped flat-leaf parsley

1 tbsp olive oil

Salt and pepper

1 In a food processor, add chickpeas, roasted red peppers, Great Northern beans, lemon zest and juice, red pepper flakes, thyme, and parsley. Purée on low until incorporated.

2 With the food processor running, drizzle in oil. Taste and season with salt and pepper and pulse once more to incorporate until smooth but not runny. Serve immediately with pita or crudité or store in an airtight container in the refrigerator for up to 2 days.

Nutrition per serving

Calories	150	Sodium	400mg
Total Fat	3g	Total Carbohydrate	23g
Saturated Fat	0g	Dietary Fiber	7g
Cholesterol	0mg	Sugars	4g
		Protein	8g

GREEN SPLIT PEA & VEGETABLE DUMPLINGS

Steamed dumplings are a fun and interactive snack to make with friends and family. Pre-made wonton wrappers make this an easy recipe to create.

● Make it with meat

Add 4 ½ ounces (130g) cooked ground pork along with cabbage and reduce cabbage to 2 cups.

MAKES 36 · PREP 35 MINS · COOK 1 HR 20 MINS

⅔ cup rice wine vinegar

⅔ cup soy sauce

½ tsp Sriracha

3 tbsp sesame oil

2 garlic cloves, minced

1 tsp grated ginger

3 green onions, finely chopped

3 cups finely shredded savoy or Napa cabbage

1 cup cooked green split peas

Pinch red pepper flakes

1 tsp mirin

Salt and pepper

½ cup chopped cilantro

1 tsp cornstarch

1 tbsp water

36 (3in; 8cm) wonton wrappers

1 To make dipping sauce, in a small bowl whisk together rice wine vinegar, soy sauce, and Sriracha. Set aside.

2 To make filling, in a large skillet heat 1 tablespoon sesame oil over medium heat until warm. Add garlic and ginger and cook for 1 to 2 minutes until soft. Add green onion and cabbage and cook for 2 to 3 minutes until cabbage begins to wilt. Add split peas, red pepper flakes, and mirin. Cook for 2 to 3 additional minutes until mixture is warmed through. Taste and season with salt and pepper. Stir in cilantro and remove from heat.

3 Prepare a clean, flat work surface to assemble dumplings. In a small bowl, whisk together cornstarch and water. Place one wonton wrapper on the work surface and place 1 scant tablespoon filling into middle of wrapper. Brush all four edges with cornstarch mixture. Fold wrapper in half and press edges together to seal, then set aside. Repeat with remaining wrappers and ingredients.

4 In one nonstick skillet, add 1 cup of water, bring to a boil, then reduce to a simmer over low heat. In another nonstick skillet, heat remaining 2 tablespoons sesame oil over medium-low heat until warm. Working in batches, pan fry dumplings in sesame oil for 2 to 3 minutes per side until golden brown. Then transfer batch to simmering water, cover, and steam for 2 minutes. Repeat with remaining dumplings. Serve immediately with soy dipping sauce.

Nutrition per dumpling

Calories	50
Total Fat	1.5g
Saturated Fat	0g
Cholesterol	0mg
Sodium	490mg
Total Carbohydrate	7g
Dietary Fiber	1g
Sugars	1g
Protein	2g

SOUPS & STEWS

TOMATILLO SOUP
WITH NAVY BEANS & CORN

Inspired by Mexican tortilla soup, this recipe has great texture from the corn and tang from the tomatillos. The creamy avocado and fresh cilantro garnish make this dish extra special.

SERVES 10 · PREP 20 MINS · COOK 50 MINS

2 tbsp vegetable oil

1 medium white onion, diced

2 large garlic cloves, minced

1 jalapeño, deseeded and
 finely diced

Pinch red pepper flakes

15 medium tomatillos, about
 1 ½ inches (4cm) in diameter

6 cups vegetable stock

Kernels from 2 white or
 yellow corn cobs

3 ½ cups cooked navy beans

Juice 2 large limes

¼ cup chopped cilantro

Salt and pepper

Cubes ripe avocado,
 to garnish

Lime wedges, to garnish

1 In a large stockpot or soup pot, heat oil over medium heat until shimmering. Add onion and cook for 3 to 4 minutes until translucent but not brown. Add garlic, jalapeño, and red pepper flakes, and cook for 2 minutes, or until soft.

2 Rinse tomatillos, remove husks, and roughly chop. Add to the pot and stir to combine. Let mixture cook for 7 to 8 minutes, covered, until tomatillos begin to soften. Stir in stock and bring mixture to a boil. Then reduce heat and simmer, covered, for 20 to 25 minutes.

3 Stir in corn, navy beans, lime juice, and cilantro. Cook for another 8 to 10 minutes to heat ingredients through. Taste and season with salt and pepper. To serve, ladle soup into bowls and garnish with avocado. Top each with a lime wedge and serve immediately.

● **Make it with meat**

Add 5 ounces (140g) cooked and shredded chicken when you stir in corn and white beans.

Why not try... For delightfully chewy texture, add ½ cup hominy along with corn, and reduce navy beans to 3 cups.

Nutrition per serving

Calories	330
Total Fat	8g
Saturated Fat	1.5g
Cholesterol	0mg
Sodium	115mg
Total Carbohydrate	55g
Dietary Fiber	15g
Sugars	6g
Protein	11g

HOPPIN' JOHN SOUP

Traditionally served in the South on New Year's Day to bring good luck, Hoppin' John soup is usually a side dish, but here it's transformed into a hearty and healthy meal.

SERVES 6 · PREP 30 MINS · COOK 40 MINS

1 tbsp olive oil

1 small yellow onion, diced

1 small red bell pepper, deseeded and diced

2 celery stalks, diced

1 garlic clove, minced

14.5oz (411g) can diced tomatoes

2 thyme sprigs

Pinch ground cayenne pepper

½ tsp smoked paprika

4 cups vegetable stock

Salt and pepper

2 cups cooked black-eyed peas

1 ½ cups cooked brown rice

½ cup chopped green onion

¼ cup chopped flat-leaf parsley

1 In a large saucepan, warm oil over medium-low heat. Add onion and cook for 2 minutes, or until it starts to become translucent. Add bell pepper and celery and cook for an additional 2 minutes. Add garlic and cook for an additional minute.

2 Incorporate tomatoes, thyme, cayenne, paprika, and stock. Bring to a boil then reduce heat to low and cook, covered, for 20 minutes. Taste and season with salt and pepper.

3 Combine black-eyed peas and rice. Cook for an additional 10 minutes, or until peas and rice are warmed through. Transfer to serving bowls and garnish with green onion and parsley.

Nutrition per serving

Calories	180
Total Fat	3g
Saturated Fat	0g
Cholesterol	0mg
Sodium	680mg
Total Carbohydrate	30g
Dietary Fiber	6g
Sugars	5g
Protein	6g

● Make it with meat

Stir in 5 ounces (140g) cooked, chopped, and smoked turkey leg or ham when adding stock and tomatoes.

LIMA BEAN BISQUE

The natural creaminess of lima beans gives this soup the texture of a bisque without the heavy cream. Serve with homemade croutons and cracked black pepper.

SERVES 4 · PREP 15 MINS · COOK 30 MINS

1 tbsp unsalted butter

1 medium yellow onion, chopped

2 celery stalks, chopped

4 cups cooked lima beans

5 cups vegetable stock

½ tsp red pepper flakes

4 thyme sprigs

2 tbsp chopped basil

2 tbsp chopped flat-leaf parsley

Salt and pepper

1 In a large stockpot or soup pot, melt butter over medium heat. Add onion and cook for 4 to 5 minutes until it starts to become translucent but not brown. Add celery and cook for an additional 3 to 4 minutes until it starts to soften.

2 Add lima beans and stir to combine. Pour in stock and bring to a boil. Add red pepper flakes and thyme, then reduce heat to a simmer. Cook, uncovered, for 15 minutes. Turn off the heat, remove thyme stems, and stir in basil and parsley. Let cool.

3 Once cool, working in batches, pour soup into a blender and purée. Return soup to the pot and reheat. Season with salt and pepper to taste. Serve immediately.

Nutrition per serving

Calories	280
Total Fat	3.5g
Saturated Fat	2g
Cholesterol	10mg
Sodium	190mg
Total Carbohydrate	46g
Dietary Fiber	15g
Sugars	10g
Protein	15g

● Make it with meat

Garnish each bowl of soup with 1 tablespoon crisp, crumbled bacon or prosciutto.

GUMBO Z'HERBES

Also known as green gumbo, Gumbo Z'herbes is a longstanding tradition in Louisiana. Classically vegetarian, it is often eaten on Good Friday, and thought to bring good luck all year long.

● Make it with meat

Add 5 ounces (140g) shredded or chopped smoked turkey.

SERVES 10 · PREP 1 HR 10 MINS · COOK 1 HR

1 bunch Swiss chard
1 bunch kale
1 bunch watercress
1 bunch mustard greens
1 bunch dandelion greens
2 cups baby spinach
1 ½ cups cooked moth beans
⅔ cup vegetable oil
⅔ cup all-purpose flour
1 medium yellow onion, diced
1 medium green bell pepper, diced
3 celery stalks, diced
1 garlic clove, minced
2 cups vegetable stock
2 bay leaves
½ tsp paprika
3 thyme sprigs
1 tsp ground cayenne pepper
2 tbsp white wine vinegar
Salt and pepper
Hot sauce, optional

1 Remove and discard tough stems and ribs from Swiss chard, kale, watercress, mustard greens, dandelion greens, and spinach leaves. Roughly chop the greens—you want approximately 2 pounds (1kg). Place greens in a large bowl and cover in cold water. Agitate to rinse dirt or grit then drain.

2 In a stockpot, bring 6 cups water to a rolling boil. Add greens and cook, covered, for 15 to 20 minutes until tender. Reserve 2 cups cooking liquid then drain cooked greens.

3 In a blender or food processor, blend together half of cooked greens, ¾ cup moth beans, and reserved cooking liquid until smooth. Set aside.

4 To make roux, in a large heavy-bottomed stockpot or Dutch oven, heat oil over medium heat. Once shimmering, add flour and stir until smooth. Reduce heat to low and stir continuously for 10 to 15 minutes until roux is the color of peanut butter and the consistency of milk.

5 Immediately stir in onion, bell pepper, and celery. Cook for 2 to 3 minutes over medium heat, stirring continuously, until mixture thickens and vegetables are coated in roux. Add garlic, stock, bay leaves, paprika, thyme, and cayenne. Pour in puréed greens and moth bean mixture and cook, covered, for 15 minutes.

6 Add remaining cooked greens and moth beans and briskly simmer for 15 minutes, covered. Stir in vinegar. Taste and season with salt and pepper. Remove bay leaf and thyme stems and serve immediately with hot sauce, if using.

Nutrition per serving

Calories	260
Total Fat	16g
Saturated Fat	10g
Cholesterol	0mg
Sodium	390mg
Total Carbohydrate	25g
Dietary Fiber	8g
Sugars	4g
Protein	8g

TOMATO & SPLIT PEA BISQUE

Smoky chipotle and fire-roasted tomatoes flavor this creamy soup.

SERVES 6 · PREP 25 MINS · COOK 45 MINS

- 1 tbsp olive oil
- 1 medium yellow onion, chopped
- 1 carrot, diced
- 1 celery stalk, diced
- 1 garlic clove, minced
- 14.5oz (411g) can fire-roasted chopped tomatoes
- 3 cups cooked yellow split peas or fava beans
- 1 chipotle in adobo, minced
- 3 cups vegetable stock
- 1 tsp ground coriander
- Juice 1 medium lime
- ⅓ cup heavy cream
- Salt and pepper

1 In a medium stockpot or Dutch oven, heat oil over medium-low heat until shimmering. Add onion, carrot, and celery and cook for 2 to 3 minutes. Add garlic and cook for 1 to 2 minutes.

2 Add fire-roasted tomatoes, split peas, chipotle in adobo, stock, and coriander. Stir to combine. Bring to a boil then reduce to a simmer and cook, covered, for 20 to 25 minutes until soup thickens. Remove from heat and let cool for 5 to 10 minutes.

3 In a blender, working in batches, purée soup until completely smooth. Return to the pot and reheat. Stir in lime juice and heavy cream. Season with salt and pepper. Serve immediately.

Nutrition per serving

Calories	230
Total Fat	8g
Saturated Fat	3.5g
Cholesterol	20mg
Sodium	380mg
Total Carbohydrate	32g
Dietary Fiber	11g
Sugars	8g
Protein	9g

● **Make it vegan**

Instead of heavy cream, use an equal amount coconut cream.

LEMON & HERB SPLIT PEA SOUP

This classic soup is lightened with fresh flavors of citrus, thyme, and basil.

SERVES 6 · PREP 20 MINS · COOK 1 HR 10 MINS

- 1 tbsp olive oil
- 1 medium yellow onion, chopped
- 1 carrot, diced
- 1 large celery stalk, diced
- 1 garlic clove, minced
- 2 cups dry split green peas
- 6 cups vegetable stock
- Pinch red pepper flakes
- 3 thyme sprigs
- ½ tbsp chopped basil
- Zest and juice 2 large lemons
- Salt and pepper

1 In a stockpot, heat oil over medium-low heat until shimmering. Add onion, carrot, and celery and cook for 2 to 3 minutes until soft. Add garlic and cook for an additional minute.

2 Add split peas, stock, red pepper flakes, and thyme. Bring to a boil then reduce heat and simmer, covered, for 45 minutes to 1 hour until split peas are tender and soup thickens, stirring frequently.

3 Stir in basil and lemon zest and juice. Taste and season with salt and pepper. Remove thyme stems and serve immediately.

Nutrition per serving

Calories	200
Total Fat	2.5g
Saturated Fat	0g
Cholesterol	0mg
Sodium	560mg
Total Carbohydrate	42g
Dietary Fiber	17g
Sugars	5g
Protein	15g

● **Make it with meat**

For a smoky complement, add 2 slices raw, chopped bacon and cook with onion.

KABOCHA SQUASH & YELLOW LENTIL SOUP

Kabocha is a winter squash with a sweet flavor and vivid orange flesh. Roasting enhances its sweetness, making it a natural companion to curry and coconut milk.

SERVES 4 · PREP 20 MINS · COOK 1 HR 40 MINS

1 medium kabocha squash, deseeded and cut into quarters

2 tbsp olive oil

1 carrot, chopped

1 yellow onion, chopped

1 celery stalk, chopped

5 cups vegetable broth

1 ½ cups dry yellow lentils

2 tsp curry powder

½ tsp ground ginger

5.6fl oz (165ml) can unsweetened coconut milk

Salt and pepper

1 medium lime, cut into 4 wedges

Unsweetened, toasted coconut flakes, to garnish

1 Preheat the oven to 350°F (180°C). Place squash quarters cut-side up on a baking sheet and drizzle with 1 tablespoon oil. Roast for 40 minutes, or until tender. Let cool.

2 Meanwhile, in a soup pot, heat remaining 1 tablespoon oil over medium heat. Add carrot, onion, and celery and cook for 3 minutes, or until translucent. Add 3 cups broth and yellow lentils and bring to a boil. Reduce to a simmer and cook, covered, for 45 minutes to an hour until lentils are tender. To ensure there is enough liquid for the lentils to absorb, add up to 2 cups additional broth as need.

3 When lentils are tender, scoop roasted kabocha away from skin and add flesh to the pot. Stir in curry powder and ginger and heat through. With a blender or immersion blender, purée until smooth. Stir in coconut milk and heat thoroughly. Season with salt and pepper to taste. Serve with a lime wedge.

● **Make it with meat**

Use chicken broth rather than vegetable broth and garnish each serving with ½ slice crumbled bacon.

Nutrition per serving

Calories	322
Total Fat	15g
Saturated Fat	8g
Cholesterol	0mg
Sodium	287mg
Total Carbohydrate	41g
Dietary Fiber	13g
Sugars	4g
Protein	8g

Pulse exchange
Instead of yellow lentils, substitute an equal amount **red lentils.**

MUNG BEAN & MISO NOODLE SOUP

This comforting traditional Asian soup gets an extra layer of texture and a boost of protein here from the addition of mung beans.

SERVES 6 · PREP 15 MINS · COOK 15 MINS

5 cups low-sodium vegetable broth

3 tbsp white miso paste

1 tbsp grated ginger

2 garlic cloves, minced

2 tbsp rice wine vinegar

2 tsp soy sauce

3oz (85g) dry Japanese udon noodles

1 ½ cups cooked mung beans

7oz (200g; about ½ block) extra firm tofu, drained, pressed, and cubed

2 cups shredded Napa or Savoy cabbage

½ cup sliced green onion, to garnish

1 In a medium Dutch oven or stockpot, combine broth, miso paste, ginger, garlic, vinegar, and soy sauce.

2 Bring mixture to a boil and add udon. Reduce heat and simmer for 5 to 6 minutes until udon start to become tender.

3 Add mung beans, tofu, and cabbage. Stir to combine thoroughly and cook for 5 minutes, or until udon are completely cooked and tofu is warmed through.

4 Transfer to serving bowls and garnish with green onion. Serve immediately.

Nutrition per serving

Calories	160
Total Fat	3g
Saturated Fat	0g
Cholesterol	0mg
Sodium	630mg
Total Carbohydrate	24g
Dietary Fiber	6g
Sugars	5g
Protein	11g

● Make it with meat

For a seafood version, add ½ pound (225g) cooked, peeled and deveined shrimp to broth along with mung beans.

GREEN MINESTRONE
WITH ARUGULA PESTO

Minestrone is a classic Italian soup of vegetables and beans. This one uses the fresh, green produce of spring, and is topped off with a dollop of vibrant homemade pesto.

● Make it with meat

Add 5 ounces (140g) cooked, cubed chicken along with vegetables in step 3 and use chicken stock rather than vegetable stock.

SERVES 6 · PREP 50 MINS · COOK 40 MINS

½ cup plus 1 tbsp olive oil

1 large leek, white and light
    green parts sliced and rinsed

1 large celery stalk, diced

1 garlic clove, minced

5 cups vegetable stock

1 bay leaf

1 thyme sprig

Pinch red pepper flakes

2 cups cooked navy beans

1 small zucchini, diced

1 cup trimmed and cut green
    beans (1-in; 3cm pieces)

1 tbsp chopped basil

1 cup frozen green peas,
    thawed

1 cup shredded savoy cabbage

½ tsp chopped oregano

Salt and pepper

1 cup baby arugula

½ cup pine nuts, toasted

1 cup grated Parmesan cheese

1 tsp grated lemon zest

1 In a medium stockpot, heat 1 tablespoon oil over medium-low heat. Add leek and cook for 2 to 3 minutes until it begins to soften. Add celery and garlic and cook for an additional 2 to 3 minutes.

2 Add stock, bay leaf, thyme, red pepper flakes, and navy beans. Bring to a boil then reduce heat and simmer, covered, for 15 minutes, or until navy beans are warmed through.

3 Add zucchini, green beans, basil, green peas, savoy cabbage, and oregano. Simmer for an additional 15 minutes, or until vegetables are tender and cooked through. Taste and season with salt and pepper.

4 Meanwhile, to make pesto, in a food processor combine arugula, pine nuts, Parmesan, and lemon zest. With processor running, slowly drizzle in remaining ½ cup oil until fully combined.

5 Remove bay leaf. Portion soup into 6 bowls and top each with ½ tablespoon pesto. Serve immediately.

Nutrition per serving

Calories	390
Total Fat	20g
Saturated Fat	5g
Cholesterol	10mg
Sodium	410mg
Total Carbohydrate	30g
Dietary Fiber	11g
Sugars	5g
Protein	15g

Pulse exchange

Substitute an equal amount **mung beans** or **Great Northern beans** rather than navy beans.

CARIBBEAN BLACK BEAN & LENTIL SOUP

Bell peppers and jalapeño flavor this comforting and slightly spicy soup, made heartier with black beans and beluga lentils.

● Make it with meat

For a natural addition, add 1 (3–4oz; 84–110g) cooked, smoked sausage along with vegetables in step 1.

SERVES 4 · PREP 25 MINS · COOK 30 MINS

1 tbsp vegetable oil

1 cup yellow onion, diced

½ cup red bell pepper, diced

½ cup green bell pepper, diced

1 small jalapeño, deseeded and minced

1 tbsp garlic, minced

4 cups vegetable stock

1 bay leaf

2 cups dry black beans, soaked

1 cup cooked Beluga lentils

1 ½ tsp allspice

¼ tsp ground cayenne pepper

½ tsp smoked paprika

Juice 2 medium limes

Salt and pepper

Chopped cilantro, to garnish

1 In a medium stockpot or Dutch oven, heat oil over medium heat. Add onion, red bell pepper, green bell pepper, and jalapeño. Cook for 4 to 5 minutes until vegetables begin to soften. Add garlic and cook for an additional 1 to 2 minutes.

2 Incorporate stock, bay leaf, black beans, Beluga lentils, allspice, cayenne, and paprika. Bring to a boil then reduce heat and simmer, covered, for 20 minutes, or until soup begins to thicken.

3 Stir in lime juice. Taste and season with salt and pepper. Remove bay leaf and garnish with cilantro before serving.

Nutrition per serving

Calories	400
Total Fat	7g
Saturated Fat	3g
Cholesterol	0mg
Sodium	150mg
Total Carbohydrate	68g
Dietary Fiber	17g
Sugars	7g
Protein	21g

Pulse exchange

Substitute an equal amount **adzuki beans** instead of black beans.

YELLOW LENTIL MULLIGATAWNY

This spicy and sweet lentil soup is an Anglo-Indian classic.

SERVES 8 · PREP 25 MINS · COOK 45 MINS

2 tbsp coconut oil

1 medium yellow onion, diced

2 celery stalks, diced

2 carrots, diced

3 garlic cloves, minced

¾ tsp curry powder

¾ tsp ground coriander

¼ tsp ground cayenne pepper

1 cup dry yellow lentils

14oz (411g) can crushed tomatoes

4 cups vegetable broth

13.5fl oz (400ml) can coconut milk

Juice 2 large limes

Salt and pepper

Chopped cilantro, to garnish

1 In a stockpot, heat coconut oil over medium-low heat. Add onion, celery, and carrots and cook for 2 to 3 minutes until soft. Add garlic and cook for an additional minute.

2 Add curry powder, coriander, and cayenne. Cook for 1 minute then stir in lentils. Add crushed tomatoes, broth, and coconut milk. Bring to a boil then reduce to a simmer and cook, covered, for 20 to 35 minutes until lentils are tender.

3 Stir in lime juice. Taste and season with salt and pepper. Transfer to serving bowls, garnish with cilantro, and serve immediately.

Nutrition per serving

Calories	200
Total Fat	9g
Saturated Fat	7g
Cholesterol	0mg
Sodium	190mg
Total Carbohydrate	24g
Dietary Fiber	6g
Sugars	6g
Protein	7g

● **Make it with meat**

For a stronger flavor, use chicken broth in place of the vegetable broth.

SPICY RED LENTIL SOUP

In this soup, chile pepper heat is balanced with smoky paprika and earthy cumin.

SERVES 4 · PREP 25 MINUTES · COOK 40 MINUTES

1 tbsp olive oil

1 large carrot, peeled and diced

1 medium yellow onion, diced

1 small green Thai chile or jalapeño, finely diced

1 cup dry red lentils

3 cups water

1 tbsp tomato paste

15oz (420g) can diced tomatoes

1 tbsp smoked paprika

2 tsp light brown sugar

2 ½ tsp ground cumin

1 tsp Sriracha

Salt and pepper

Chopped green onions, to garnish

1 In a large stockpot, heat oil over medium heat until shimmering. Add carrot and onion and cook for 4 to 5 minutes until soft. Add chile and cook for an additional 1 to 2 minutes. Incorporate lentils.

2 Add water, tomato paste, diced tomatoes, paprika, brown sugar, cumin, and Sriracha. Bring to a boil then reduce heat and simmer, covered, for 35 to 40 minutes until vegetables and lentils are cooked.

3 Taste and season with salt and pepper. Transfer to serving bowls and garnish with green onions. Serve immediately.

Nutrition per serving

Calories	240
Total Fat	3.5g
Saturated Fat	0.5g
Cholesterol	0mg
Sodium	260mg
Total Carbohydrate	40g
Dietary Fiber	10g
Sugars	9g
Protein	13g

● **Make it with meat**

For a smoky complement, add 2 slices of bacon and sauté with the carrot and onion.

PIGEON PEA & PUMPKIN CHILI

Pumpkin may seem like an unusual ingredient in chili, but its sweetness is a lovely complement to this soup's spice.

SERVES 6 · PREP 25 MINS · COOK 45 MINS

1 tbsp olive oil

1 small yellow onion, diced

2 garlic cloves, minced

1 small jalapeño, deseeded and minced

14oz (411g) can diced tomatoes

2 ½ tsp ground cumin

1 ½ tsp chipotle chili powder

2 cups vegetable stock

2 ½ cups cooked pigeon peas

2 cups cooked adzuki beans

1 cup corn kernels

15oz (425g) can 100 percent pure pumpkin

Salt and pepper

¾ cup chopped cilantro, to garnish

1 In a large stockpot, heat oil over medium-low heat. Add onion and cook for 2 to 3 minutes until soft. Add garlic and jalapeño and cook for an additional minute.

2 Incorporate diced tomatoes, cumin, and chipotle chili powder. Stir in stock, bring to a boil, then reduce heat and simmer for 5 minutes. Stir in pigeon peas, adzuki beans, and corn. Bring to a boil then reduce heat to low and simmer, covered, for an additional 20 minutes.

3 Fold in pumpkin and stir to combine. Cook, covered, for an additional 10 minutes. Taste and season with salt and pepper. Transfer to 6 serving bowls, garnish with 2 tablespoons cilantro, and serve immediately.

Nutrition per serving

Calories	360
Total Fat	4g
Saturated Fat	0.5g
Cholesterol	0mg
Sodium	180mg
Total Carbohydrate	68g
Dietary Fiber	16g
Sugars	9g
Protein	15g

● **Make it with meat**

Cook ½ pound (225g) raw, ground turkey along with onion in step 1.

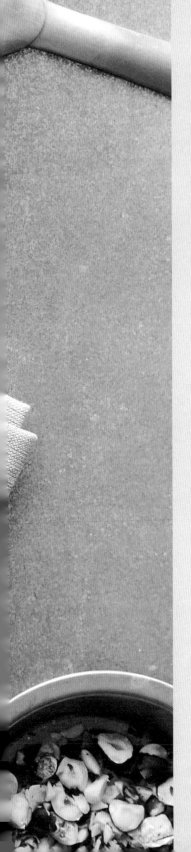

CHICKPEA & NAVY BEAN BISQUE

While not a traditional bisque, this soup certainly seems like one with its silky, rich texture. This simple, elegant recipe makes an excellent first course for a dinner party.

SERVES 4 · PREP 15 MINS · COOK 30 MINS

½ tbsp olive oil, plus extra to garnish

1 leek, white parts only, sliced and rinsed

1 garlic clove, minced

1 tbsp dry vermouth

3 cups vegetable stock

2 cups cooked navy beans

1 cup cooked chickpeas

¼ cup heavy cream

Salt and pepper

Chopped, toasted hazelnut, to garnish

1 In a Dutch oven or large pot, warm oil over medium-low heat until shimmering. Add leek and cook for 4 to 5 minutes until soft and translucent. Add garlic and cook for an additional 2 minutes.

2 Add vermouth and cook for 1 to 2 minutes. Incorporate stock, navy beans, and chickpeas. Bring to a boil then reduce to a simmer and cook, covered, for 15 minutes. Remove from heat and let cool for 5 to 10 minutes until safe to use in a blender.

3 Transfer mixture to a blender and purée until smooth. Return to the pot over medium heat, stir in heavy cream, and heat. Taste and season with salt and pepper. Transfer to serving bowls, garnish with hazelnut and a swirl of oil, and serve immediately.

Nutrition per serving

Calories	270
Total Fat	6g
Saturated Fat	2g
Cholesterol	10mg
Sodium	390mg
Total Carbohydrate	41g
Dietary Fiber	14g
Sugars	5g
Protein	12g

● **Make it vegan**

The cooked chickpeas are naturally creamy, so omit heavy cream for a vegan-friendly version.

PIGEON PEA, QUINOA, & KALE SOUP

This soup is hearty and filling without being heavy. It's also a nutritional powerhouse, with a trifecta of superfood ingredients providing vitamins, fiber, and protein.

SERVES 4 · PREP 25 MINS · COOK 45 MINS

1 tbsp olive oil
1 small yellow onion, diced
1 large carrot, diced
1 celery stalk, diced
1 garlic clove, minced
Pinch red pepper flakes
Leaves 3 thyme sprigs
1 bay leaf
7 cups vegetable stock
14.5oz (411g) can diced tomatoes
1 cup dry tri-color quinoa
2 cups cooked pigeon peas
2 cups chopped kale
Salt and pepper

1 In a large Dutch oven or soup pot, warm oil over medium heat until shimmering. Add onion, carrot, and celery and cook for 4 minutes, or until tender but not brown. Add garlic and cook for an additional 2 minutes.

2 Add red pepper flakes, thyme, and bay leaf. Stir to combine and cook for 1 minute. Incorporate stock and diced tomatoes. Bring to a boil then add quinoa. Reduce heat to low and cook, partially covered, for 25 minutes, or until quinoa is fully cooked.

3 Stir in pigeon peas and kale. Cook for an additional 10 minutes, or until kale is tender. Taste and season with salt and pepper. Remove bay leaf and serve immediately.

Nutrition per serving

Calories	380
Total Fat	7g
Saturated Fat	0.5g
Cholesterol	0mg
Sodium	740mg
Total Carbohydrate	67g
Dietary Fiber	15g
Sugars	14g
Protein	15g

● Make it with meat

Remove casings from 2 links mild Italian sausage. Crumble and brown alongside garlic.

SOUTHWEST NAVY BEAN SOUP

This soup has the vivid flavors of chili, lime, and cilantro with a light, brothy texture.

SERVES 6 · PREP 10 MINS · COOK 1 HR 10 MINS

- 1 tbsp olive oil
- 1 medium yellow onion, diced
- 1 small jalapeño, deseeded and diced
- 1 garlic clove, minced
- 4 ½ cups vegetable stock
- 1 tsp ground cumin
- 1 tsp smoked paprika
- 1 tsp dried oregano leaves
- 1 tsp ancho chili powder
- 3 cups soaked navy beans
- Juice 1 lime
- 1 tbsp chopped cilantro
- Salt and pepper

1 In a large soup pot, heat oil over medium-low heat. Add onion and jalapeño and cook for 2 to 3 minutes. Add garlic and cook for 1 to 2 minutes.

2 Incorporate stock, cumin, paprika, oregano, and chili powder. Add navy beans and stir to combine. Bring to a boil then reduce heat and simmer, covered, for 45 minutes to 1 hour until beans are completely tender.

3 In a blender, purée ¾ cup soup until smooth. Return to the pot and stir to combine.

4 Stir in lime juice and cilantro. Taste and season with salt and pepper. Serve immediately.

Nutrition per serving

Calories		280
Total Fat		3.5g
Saturated Fat		0g
Cholesterol		0mg
Sodium		290mg
Total Carbohydrate		47g
Dietary Fiber		18g
Sugars		5g
Protein		16g

● **Make it with meat**

Ham naturally complements navy beans. Add 2 ounces (55g) chopped, cooked ham along with beans.

FEIJOADA

This simple Brazilian stew, often a celebratory dish, is prepared on weekends when there is time to cook it low and slow.

SERVES 4 · PREP 20 MINS · COOK 1 HR

- 1 tbsp olive oil
- 1 medium red onion, chopped
- 1 celery stalk, chopped
- 1 red or yellow bell pepper, deseeded and chopped
- 4 garlic cloves, minced
- 2 thyme sprigs
- 2 large tomatoes, deseeded and chopped
- 3 cups cooked black beans
- 3 cups vegetable stock
- 1 chipotle chile in adobo, minced
- Juice 1 lime
- Salt and pepper
- ¼ cup chopped parsley, to garnish

1 In a medium stockpot, heat oil over medium-high heat. Add onion, celery, and bell pepper. Cook, partially covered, for 5 to 6 minutes until soft. Add garlic and cook for an additional 1 to 2 minutes.

2 Stir in thyme, tomatoes, black beans, stock, and chipotle chile in adobo. Bring to a boil then reduce heat and simmer, covered, for 45 minutes, stirring occasionally.

3 Remove from heat and stir in lime juice. Taste and season with salt and pepper. Garnish with parsley and serve immediately.

Nutrition per serving

Calories		280
Total Fat		5g
Saturated Fat		0.5g
Cholesterol		0mg
Sodium		580mg
Total Carbohydrate		45g
Dietary Fiber		16g
Sugars		10g
Protein		14g

● **Make it with meat**

For more traditional Feijoada, chop 1 (3–4oz; 85–110g) cooked, smoked sausage and add along with black beans in step 2.

MUNG BEAN GREEN GAZPACHO

Green gazpacho is a unique spin on the classic Spanish cold soup. It's best served ice cold, so don't skimp on the refrigeration time.

SERVES 4 · PREP 30 MINS

2 cups packed arugula

1 medium cucumber, peeled, deseeded, and chopped

1 garlic clove

¾ cup cooked mung beans

¼ cup roughly chopped cilantro

¼ cup mint leaves

3 green onions, white and light green parts chopped

1 avocado, halved and pitted

1 tbsp olive oil

2 tsp red wine vinegar

Juice 1 large lemon

1 ¼ cups cold water

Salt and pepper

2 tbsp chopped chives

¼ cup sprouted mung beans

1 In a food processor, combine arugula, cucumber, garlic, mung beans, cilantro, mint, and green onion. Blend on high until finely chopped.

2 Add avocado, oil, vinegar, and lemon juice. Process on high while slowly incorporating cold water. Taste and season with salt and pepper and pulse once more to combine.

3 Transfer to an airtight container and refrigerate for at least 2 hours until chilled. Portion gazpacho into four serving bowls and garnish with ½ tablespoon chopped chives and 1 tablespoon sprouted mung beans.

● **Make it with meat**

Sauté 1 pound (450g) peeled and deveined shrimp and garlic, and add atop each serving.

Nutrition per serving

Calories	180
Total Fat	12g
Saturated Fat	2g
Cholesterol	0mg
Sodium	580mg
Total Carbohydrate	17g
Dietary Fiber	8g
Sugars	5g
Protein	6g

Why not try...

Garnish each serving with 1 tablespoon diced, ripe avocado and a drizzle extra virgin olive oil.

CREAMY SPINACH & MUNG BEAN SOUP

This soup is everything you love about creamed spinach. Don't let the bright color fool you—it's as luxurious as it is good for you, so sop it up with freshly baked bread.

SERVES 4 · PREP 25 MINS · COOK 40 MINS

1 tbsp unsalted butter

1 medium yellow onion, diced

1 garlic clove, minced

1 medium russet potato, peeled and cut into ½-inch (1cm) chunks

3 cups vegetable broth

6oz (170g) bag baby spinach

1 cup cooked mung beans

2 tbsp dry sherry

⅛ tsp ground cayenne pepper

⅛ tsp ground nutmeg

Salt and pepper

¼ cup grated Parmesan cheese

1 In a Dutch oven, melt butter over medium heat. Add onion and cook for 3 to 4 minutes until translucent. Add garlic and cook for 2 minutes.

2 Add potato and stir to combine. Cook for 2 to 3 minutes. Add 2 cups broth and bring to a boil. Reduce heat to a simmer and cook, covered, for 12 to 15 minutes until potatoes are fork tender.

3 Add spinach and mung beans and cook for an additional 5 minutes, or until spinach wilts and mung beans are warmed through. Let cool until safe to use in a blender.

4 With a high-powered blender or immersion blender, purée soup until completely smooth. (If using a blender, you may have to work in batches.) Return puréed mixture to the pot and stir in sherry, cayenne, and nutmeg. For a thinner consistency, add up to 1 cup remaining broth. Taste and season with salt and pepper.

5 Reheat soup over medium heat. Transfer to serving bowls and top with Parmesan. Serve immediately.

Nutrition per serving

Calories	180
Total Fat	5g
Saturated Fat	3g
Cholesterol	15mg
Sodium	800mg
Total Carbohydrate	25g
Dietary Fiber	6g
Sugars	4g
Protein	8g

Make it vegan
Replace butter with an equal amount coconut oil.

Make it with meat
Crumble 1 tablespoon crisp prosciutto on top of each bowl of soup.

Why not try...
Garnish with flat-leaf parsley or watercress for more pronounced green flavor.

PINTO BEAN PEANUT STEW

Peanut soups and stews are a staple in areas of Africa. This unusual dish combines creamy peanut butter with beans and bitter greens for a hearty stew.

SERVES 6 · PREP 25 MINS · COOK 45 MINS

1 tbsp coconut oil

1 small yellow onion, chopped

1 garlic clove, minced

1 large sweet potato, peeled and cut into 1-in (3cm) cubes

1 tsp ancho chili powder

½ tsp ground cayenne pepper

14.5oz (411g) can crushed tomatoes

2 ½ cups vegetable broth

½ cup creamy peanut butter

3 cups cooked pinto beans

3 cups chopped mustard greens

Salt and pepper

Chopped cilantro, to garnish

1 In a medium stockpot, heat coconut oil over medium-low heat until shimmering. Add yellow onion and cook for 2 to 3 minutes until soft. Add garlic and cook for 1 minute.

2 Add sweet potato, ancho chili powder, and cayenne. Stir to combine. Pour in crushed tomatoes and broth. Bring to a boil then reduce to a simmer and cook, uncovered, for 5 minutes.

3 Stir in peanut butter. Return to a boil then reduce heat and simmer, covered, for 10 minutes.

4 Fold in pinto beans and mustard greens. Return to a boil once more, then reduce to a simmer and cook, covered, for 15 minutes, or until mustard greens are tender. Taste and season with salt and pepper. Garnish with cilantro and serve immediately.

● **Make it with meat**

Add 7 ounces (200g) raw, smoked andouille sausage, diced, along with onion in step 1.

Nutrition per serving

Calories	330
Total Fat	14g
Saturated Fat	4.5g
Cholesterol	0mg
Sodium	220mg
Total Carbohydrate	40g
Dietary Fiber	13g
Sugars	8g
Protein	16g

Pulse exchange

Instead of pinto beans, substitute an equal amount **borlotti beans** or **black beans**.

SALADS
& SIDES

THREE BEAN SALAD STUFFED AVOCADOS

These stuffed avocados are filled with the Southwest flavors of corn and cilantro and are a beautiful presentation. The three beans are a protein dream and the avocado is a wonderful source of healthy fats.

SERVES 8 · PREP 20 MINS · COOK 15 MINS

1 yellow or white corn cob

½ cup cooked black beans

½ cup cooked pigeon peas

½ cup cooked mung beans or sprouted mung beans

½ cup cooked farro

1 orange or yellow bell pepper, diced

3 tbsp sour cream

¼ tsp smoked paprika

½ tsp ground cumin

1 tsp red wine vinegar

Juice 2 medium limes

1 tbsp olive oil

Salt and pepper

4 ripe avocados

½ cup chopped cilantro

1 With a grill or gas burner, char corn cob for 1 to 2 minutes per side until slightly blackened. Let cool slightly.

2 Meanwhile, in a large mixing bowl, combine black beans, pigeon peas, mung beans, farro, and bell pepper. Carefully slice kernels from cob and add to mixture.

3 To make dressing, in a small bowl whisk together sour cream, paprika, cumin, vinegar, and lime juice. Drizzle in olive oil and whisk to combine thoroughly.

4 Pour dressing over the bean mixture and toss to coat. Taste and season with salt and pepper.

5 Cut each avocado in half lengthwise and remove pits. Mound an equal amount bean mixture into center of each. Place on serving plates and garnish with cilantro.

Nutrition per serving

Calories	310
Total Fat	18g
Saturated Fat	3.5g
Cholesterol	0mg
Sodium	300mg
Total Carbohydrate	34g
Dietary Fiber	12g
Sugars	5g
Protein	8g

● **Make it with meat**

Fold 2 ½ ounces (70g) shredded rotisserie chicken into bean mixture in step 2.

BLACK GRAM & KALE SALAD
WITH MISO TAHINI DRESSING

● **Make it with meat**

To transform this salad into an entrée, add 3 ounces (85g) cooked, sliced chicken breast to each portion.

Loaded with texture, this salad is unlike most green salads. The chewy kale, crunchy coconut, creamy beans, and tangy dressing are a dynamic combination.

SERVES 6 · PREP 35 MINS

3 tbsp tahini

1 ½ tbsp miso paste

Juice 1 large lime

1 tsp soy sauce

2 tsp honey

2 tbsp rice wine vinegar

¼ tsp red pepper flakes

¼ cup cold water

1 bunch kale, tough stems removed and chopped (about 6 cups)

1 cup unsweetened, shredded coconut, toasted

1 cup cooked black gram

Salt and pepper

1 In a small nonstick skillet, toast shredded coconut over medium-low heat for 4 to 5 minutes until lightly golden brown. Immediately remove from heat and let cool completely.

2 To make dressing, in a small mixing bowl, combine tahini, miso paste, lime juice, soy sauce, honey, rice wine vinegar, and red pepper flakes. Add water and whisk until smooth.

3 In a large salad bowl, add chopped kale and about ¾ cup dressing. With your hands, massage dressing into kale for 1 to 2 minutes until kale tenderizes slightly.

4 Add toasted coconut and black gram and toss to combine. Season with salt and pepper. Serve immediately.

Nutrition per serving

Calories	210
Total Fat	13g
Saturated Fat	8g
Cholesterol	0mg
Sodium	370mg
Total Carbohydrate	19g
Dietary Fiber	7g
Sugars	5g
Protein	8g

Pulse exchange

Use an equal amount **moth beans** instead of black gram.

ROASTED BROCCOLINI & GREEN LENTIL SALAD

Roasting broccolini highlights the vegetable's best qualities—slight bitterness, a hint of sweetness, and great texture.

● **Make it with meat**

For a wonderful, salty element, garnish with 3 tablespoons crisp, crumbled prosciutto.

SERVES 6 · PREP 20 MINS · COOK 15 MINS

Juice 1 large lemon

1 tsp thyme leaves

2 tbsp lemon zest

1 tbsp Dijon mustard

1 tbsp honey

⅔ cup plus 1 tbsp olive oil

1lb (450g) broccolini

1 garlic clove, minced

¼ tsp red pepper flakes

Salt and pepper

2 cups cooked green or Le Puy lentils

1 To make dressing, in a small bowl, mix together lemon juice, thyme, 1 tablespoon lemon zest, Dijon mustard, honey, and ⅔ cup oil. Whisk until completely emulsified and set aside.

2 Preheat the oven to 350°F (180°C). Trim woody ends from broccolini, and cut each floret into 2 to 4 bite-sized pieces.

3 On a rimmed baking sheet, toss broccolini, garlic, red pepper flakes, remaining 1 tablespoon lemon zest, and remaining 1 tablespoon olive oil. Spread in an even layer and roast for 10 to 15 minutes until broccolini is tender and slightly charred.

4 In a medium mixing bowl, toss lentils and vinaigrette. On a serving platter, spread dressed lentils in an even layer and top with roasted broccolini. Season with salt and pepper to taste. Serve immediately.

Nutrition per serving

Calories	150
Total Fat	0g
Saturated Fat	0g
Cholesterol	0mg
Sodium	360mg
Total Carbohydrate	27g
Dietary Fiber	9g
Sugars	8g
Protein	11g

Why not try...

Instead of broccolini, use 1 pound (450g) long broccoli florets. Roast for 20 minutes, or until tender and slightly charred.

ROASTED CARROTS & CHICKPEAS
WITH VADOUVAN YOGURT

Vadouvan is a curry spice blend originating from Southern India. Cool yogurt tempers the spice and pairs well with the sweetness of roasted carrots.

SERVES 4 · PREP 15 MINS · COOK 30 MINS

1lb (450g) whole young carrots, leafy tops chopped and reserved for garnish

2 tbsp olive oil

2 cups cooked chickpeas

2 tsp red wine vinegar

1 garlic clove, minced

1 tsp thyme leaves

Pinch red pepper flakes

Salt and pepper

¾ cup plain Greek yogurt

1 tbsp vadouvan

1 Preheat the oven to 350°F (150°C). Arrange carrots in a single layer on a rimmed baking sheet and drizzle with olive oil. Roast for 25 to 30 minutes until fork tender.

2 Meanwhile, in a separate small mixing bowl, toss together chickpeas, vinegar, garlic, thyme, and red pepper flakes. Taste and season with salt and pepper. Set aside.

3 In a small mixing bowl, stir together Greek yogurt and vadouvan.

4 Spread yogurt on a serving platter, arrange roasted carrots over yogurt, and top with chickpea mixture. Garnish with pepper and reserved carrot leaves. Serve immediately.

Nutrition per serving

Calories	270
Total Fat	9g
Saturated Fat	1.5g
Cholesterol	<5mg
Sodium	230mg
Total Carbohydrate	37g
Dietary Fiber	7g
Sugars	12g
Protein	11g

● **Make it vegan**

Substitute an equal amount plain soy yogurt rather than Greek yogurt.

LENTIL & CAULIFLOWER TABBOULEH

Using cauliflower to make "rice" or "grains" is an easy hack that adds nutrition without sacrificing flavor. Here, it works beautifully with fresh mint and herbs in this Middle Eastern salad.

SERVES 8 · PREP 25 MINS

1 small cauliflower head

1 cup chopped flat-leaf parsley

1 cup chopped curly parsley

1 cup diced, seedless cucumber

1 cup diced tomato

1 small bunch green onions, white and green parts removed, thinly sliced

1 cup cooked brown lentils

½ cup chopped mint

Zest and juice 2 lemons

2 tbsp olive oil

Salt and pepper

1 Remove outer leaves from cauliflower head and break into florets. Place in a food processor and pulse 6 to 7 times until cauliflower resembles rice or bulgar.

2 In a large mixing bowl, combine cauliflower, flat-leaf parsley, curly parsley, cucumber, tomato, green onion, lentils, and mint. Add lemon zest and juice and olive oil and toss to combine. Taste and season with salt and pepper. Transfer to a serving dish and serve immediately.

Nutrition per serving

Calories	83
Total Fat	4g
Saturated Fat	0.5g
Cholesterol	0mg
Sodium	310mg
Total Carbohydrate	11g
Dietary Fiber	3g
Sugars	2g
Protein	4g

● **Make it with meat**

Top each serving with 3 ounces (85g) grilled steak slices.

MUNG BEAN GADO GADO

Gado Gado is an Indonesian chopped salad whose name means *mix mix*. It's always served with spicy peanut dressing, and here accompanied by crisp vegetables and pulses.

SERVES 4 · PREP 45 MINS

½ cup creamy peanut butter

1 tsp garlic powder

1 ½ tsp ground ginger

1 tsp red pepper flakes

1 ½ tsp soy sauce

Juice 2 limes

1 tsp rice wine vinegar

¾ cup water

1 small beet, peeled

2 cups shredded Savoy cabbage

½ cup cooked mung beans

½ cup halved cherry tomatoes

½ cup sprouted mung beans

½ cup chopped green beans, blanched and drained

2 hard boiled eggs, quartered

1 To make spicy peanut dressing, in a small bowl, whisk together peanut butter, garlic powder, ginger, red pepper flakes, soy sauce, lime juice, and vinegar. Stir in water until thoroughly mixed. Set aside.

2 Adjust a spiralizer to the thinnest blade and spiralize beet.

3 On a large serving platter, spread cabbage in an even layer. In separate piles atop cabbage, arrange cooked mung beans, cherry tomatoes, sprouted mung beans, spiralized beet, green beans, and hard-boiled eggs. Serve immediately with dressing on the side.

● Make it vegan

Replace hard-boiled egg with 1 cup cubed and seared tempeh or tofu.

● Make it with meat

On the serving platter, include a pile of 6 ounces (170g) thinly sliced, pan-seared steak.

Nutrition per serving

Calories	360
Total Fat	24g
Saturated Fat	0g
Cholesterol	255mg
Sodium	390mg
Total Carbohydrate	21g
Dietary Fiber	21g
Sugars	8g
Protein	21g

Pulse exchange

Use an equal amount **chickpeas** in place of cooked mung beans.

GREEN GODDESS MASON JAR SALADS

Mason jar salads are an instantly portable way to prep healthy lunches in advance. Layering the dressing on the bottom keeps the vegetables crisp until lunch time.

MAKES 2 · PREP 30 MINS

1 cup basil leaves

3 tbsp tarragon leaves

2 tbsp minced chives

¼ cup mayonnaise

½ cup plain Greek yogurt

Zest and juice 1 lemon

Salt and pepper

1 ⅓ cups chopped kale

1 medium zucchini

½ cup sprouted mung beans

½ cup sliced radishes

1 To make dressing, in a blender combine basil, tarragon, chives, mayonnaise, Greek yogurt, and lemon zest and juice. Blend until smooth. Taste and season with salt and pepper, and pulse once more to combine. (This makes more dressing than needed—store remainder in an airtight container in the refrigerator for up to 3 days.)

2 Cut both ends off zucchini. Adjust a spiralizer to the thickest blade and spiralize zucchini. With kitchen shears, roughly cut into bite-sized sections.

3 To assemble, in 2 wide-mouthed, 16-ounce (475ml) jars with lids, add 2 tablespoons dressing into the bottom of each. Then layer each with equal amounts kale, radishes, and sprouted mung beans. Top each with half of spiralized zucchini. Secure the lids. Serve immediately or store in the refrigerator for up to 2 days.

● **Make it with meat**

Layer 1 ounce (25g) cooked, shredded chicken or sliced turkey in each jar atop zucchini.

Nutrition per jar

Calories	270
Total Fat	22g
Saturated Fat	3.5g
Cholesterol	15mg
Sodium	230mg
Total Carbohydrate	12g
Dietary Fiber	3g
Sugars	5g
Protein	10g

Pulse exchange

Use an equal amount cooked **chickpeas** instead of sprouted mung beans.

VEGGIE NOODLE & LENTIL SALAD

Spiralized zucchini and carrots act as soba noodles in this light and refreshing salad.

SERVES 6 · PREP 10 MINS · COOK 20 MINS

Juice 2 large limes
2 tbsp soy sauce
1 ½ tsp grated ginger
1 ¼ tbsp sesame oil
Salt and pepper
2 large zucchini
1 large carrot

½ cup cooked and cooled Beluga lentils
3 green onions, chopped
½ cup roughly chopped cilantro
2 tbsp toasted sesame seeds

1 To make dressing, in a small bowl, whisk together lime juice, soy sauce, grated ginger, and sesame oil. Taste and season with salt and pepper. Set aside.

2 Cut both ends off zucchinis. Adjust a spiralizer to the medium blade and spiralize zucchini. Add to a large mixing bowl. Spiralize carrot and add to the mixing bowl. With kitchen shears, trim vegetables into shorter lengths.

3 Incorporate Beluga lentils and green onions. Drizzle dressing over salad and toss to combine. Garnish with cilantro and toasted sesame seeds. Serve immediately.

Nutrition per serving

Calories	100
Total Fat	4g
Saturated Fat	0.5g
Cholesterol	0mg
Sodium	560mg
Total Carbohydrate	13g
Dietary Fiber	4g
Sugars	3g
Protein	5g

●Make it vegan

Rather than soy sauce, substitute an equal amount liquid aminos.

RADICCHIO & BEAN SALAD

Radicchio's mild bitterness perfectly matches creamy navy beans in this chopped salad.

SERVES 6 · PREP 25 MINS

½ cup plus 2 tbsp parsley leaves
¼ cup basil leaves
1 large garlic clove
1 tsp Dijon mustard
2 tbsp white balsamic vinegar
1 tsp honey

⅓ cup olive oil
Salt and pepper
2 cups cooked navy beans
1 small head radicchio
4oz (110g) feta cheese, crumbled

1 To make dressing, in a food processor, combine ½ cup parsley, basil, garlic, Dijon mustard, vinegar, and honey. With the food processor running, drizzle in oil and process until smooth. Taste and season with salt and pepper.

2 In a large mixing bowl, combine navy beans and dressing and stir to thoroughly coat.

3 Discard core and outer leaves from head of radicchio. Rinse and drain the leaves. Roughly chop, add to the mixing bowl, and toss to combine.

4 Transfer mixture to a large serving platter. Garnish with crumbled feta and remaining 2 tablespoons parsley leaves. Serve immediately.

Nutrition per serving

Calories	250
Total Fat	15g
Saturated Fat	4.5g
Cholesterol	20mg
Sodium	200mg
Total Carbohydrate	20g
Dietary Fiber	7g
Sugars	3g
Protein	8g

●Make it with meat

Crisp 4 ounces (100g) prosciutto and crumble over top along with feta.

LARB CABBAGE CUPS
WITH SPROUTS & TOFU

Crisp cabbage cups are the perfect vessel for the bold, umami-packed flavors of larb. Sprouted lentils and mung beans add a unique twist to this vegetarian version of the classic Thai dish.

● Make it
with meat

For a more traditional larb, replace tofu with ¾ pound (340g) cooked ground chicken or duck.

MAKES 8 · PREP 30 MINS · COOK 20 MINS

Juice 3 large limes

2 tbsp rice wine vinegar

2 garlic cloves, minced

1 tsp grated ginger

2 tbsp soy sauce

2 Thai red chiles, deseeded and finely minced

2 ½ tbsp sesame oil

12oz (340g) extra firm cotton tofu, drained

1 cup sprouted brown lentils

1 cup sprouted mung beans

⅓ cup chopped mint

⅓ cup chopped cilantro

8 small leaves Savoy cabbage or iceberg lettuce

½ cup chopped, roasted, unsalted peanuts

1 To make dressing, in a large mixing bowl, whisk together lime juice, vinegar, garlic, ginger, soy sauce, and chiles. Set aside.

2 With a paper towel, blot tofu to absorb moisture, then roughly chop. In a medium skillet, warm sesame oil over medium heat. Add tofu. With a spatula or wooden spoon, break into small crumbles. Cook for 10 to 12 minutes until dry and lightly browned.

3 In the large mixing bowl, combine tofu and dressing. Add sprouted lentils, sprouted mung beans, mint, and cilantro. Stir to combine. Add about ½ cup tofu mixture into each cabbage leaf. Garnish with a sprinkle chopped peanuts. Serve immediately.

Nutrition per cabbage cup

Calories	180
Total Fat	11g
Saturated Fat	1.5g
Cholesterol	0mg
Sodium	280mg
Total Carbohydrate	12g
Dietary Fiber	5g
Sugars	4g
Protein	9g

Pulse exchange
Use 1 ½ cups cooked **mung beans** instead of sprouted mung beans.

ROASTED TOMATOES & WHITE BEANS
WITH BASIL VINAIGRETTE

Roasted tomatoes are lush and flavorful. Here they combine with a fresh and healthful green vinaigrette for a tasty side.

SERVES 4 · PREP 15 MINS · COOK 30 MINS

4 Roma tomatoes
3 tbsp extra virgin olive oil
2 garlic cloves, minced
1 ½ cups basil leaves
¼ cup white wine or
  champagne vinegar
Salt and pepper
2 cups cooked Great Northern
  or flageolet beans

1 Preheat the oven to 400°F (200°C). Cut tomatoes in half lengthwise and toss with minced garlic and 1 tablespoon oil. Arrange on a rimmed baking sheet and roast for 30 minutes. Let cool to room temperature.

2 Meanwhile, to make basil vinaigrette, in a blender or food processor, combine basil and vinegar. Running on low, drizzle in remaining 2 tablespoons oil until emulsified. Taste and season with salt and pepper.

3 In a separate mixing bowl, toss Great Northern beans with 2 tablespoons dressing and spread on a serving platter. Arrange roasted tomatoes on top. Season with salt and pepper to taste. Garnish with any remaining dressing and basil leaves. Serve immediately.

Nutrition per serving

Calories	214
Total Fat	10g
Saturated Fat	1.5g
Cholesterol	0mg
Sodium	591mg
Total Carbohydrate	22g
Dietary Fiber	7g
Sugars	1.7g
Protein	8.5g

● **Make it with meat**

Add ¼ pound (115g) grilled shrimp atop white beans.

TOMATO LENTIL SALAD
WITH GRILLED HALLOUMI

Halloumi is a Cypriot cheese that's easily grilled or fried. The contrasting textures of the toothsome lentils and soft grilled cheese make this salad extra special.

SERVES 4 · PREP 20 MINS · COOK 15 MINS

1 small shallot, diced

1 large garlic clove, minced

Juice and zest 1 lemon

1 tsp chopped thyme

1 tsp chopped oregano

2 tbsp olive oil

3 cups cooked green or Le Puy lentils

2 cups halved cherry or grape tomatoes

Salt and pepper

8oz (225g) halloumi cheese

1 In a medium mixing bowl, whisk together shallot, garlic, lemon juice and zest, thyme, oregano, and oil. Add lentils and tomatoes. Let marinate while you grill halloumi.

2 Heat a large nonstick skillet or grill pan over medium heat. Slice halloumi into 8 equal slices and place in the skillet. Grill for 2 to 3 minutes on each side until browned and soft.

3 Arrange lentil-tomato mixture on a serving platter and top with slices warm halloumi. Serve immediately.

● **Make it with meat**

Add 2 ounces (55g) cooked, sliced Spanish chorizo to lentil salad.

Nutrition per serving

Calories	451
Total Fat	22g
Saturated Fat	11g
Cholesterol	38mg
Sodium	843mg
Total Carbohydrate	42g
Dietary Fiber	12g
Sugars	4g
Protein	26g

Pulse exchange

If you don't have green or Le Puy lentils, use an equal amount **brown lentils** instead.

MOTH BEANS & GRILLED ROMAINE
WITH RED PEPPER VINAIGRETTE

Grilled lettuce may seem unusual, but it adds a deliciously faint smoky flavor and a layer of depth to green salads.

SERVES 6 · PREP 20 MINS · COOK 20 MINS

1 cup roasted red bell peppers, drained

1 large garlic clove

1 tbsp red wine vinegar

½ tsp chopped oregano

1 tsp chopped basil

3 tbsp olive oil

Salt and pepper

3 Romaine lettuce hearts

⅔ cup cooked moth beans

4oz (110g) soft goat cheese

1 In a food processor, combine red bell peppers, garlic, vinegar, oregano, and basil. With the processor running, drizzle in 2 tablespoons oil. Taste and season with salt and pepper.

2 Carefully cut each Romaine heart in half lengthwise, leaving as much of core intact as possible. Drizzle lettuce with remaining 1 tablespoon oil. On a grill or preheated grill pan, cook Romaine halves for 1 to 3 minutes on each side until slightly wilted and charred but not cooked through.

3 Arrange grilled lettuce on a large serving platter. Scatter mung beans evenly across top. Crumble goat cheese over mung beans. Top with dressing, to taste. Garnish with pepper and serve immediately.

● **Make it vegan**

Omit goat cheese and substitute a nut-based vegan cheese alternative.

● **Make it with meat**

Top with 4 ½ ounces (130g) cooked, shredded chicken or turkey before adding cheese.

Nutrition per serving

Calories	200
Total Fat	13g
Saturated Fat	5g
Cholesterol	15mg
Sodium	390mg
Total Carbohydrate	14g
Dietary Fiber	7g
Sugars	4g
Protein	9g

Why not try... For an extra briny kick, garnish salad with 3 to 4 tablespoons capers.

SWEET POTATO & BELUGA LENTIL SALAD
DRESSED WITH HONEY & LEMON

The nuttiness and slight tooth of the lentils mixed with the soft, caramelized sweet potato is a wonderful play of flavors and textures.

SERVES 2 · PREP 25 MINS, PLUS COOLING · COOK 45 MINS

1 large sweet potato, peeled and cubed

Dash smoked paprika

2 tbsp olive oil

Salt and pepper

3 cups water

1 ½ cups dry beluga lentils

2 green onions, white and green parts, thinly sliced

1 large celery stalk, diced, leafy parts reserved for garnish

¼ cup crumbled feta cheese

1 tbsp honey or agave nectar

Juice 1 medium lemon

1 Preheat the oven to 350°F (180°C). On a rimmed baking sheet, toss sweet potato and paprika in 1 tablespoon oil. Season with salt and pepper to taste. Roast until tender and slightly caramelized, about 25 minutes, stirring once halfway. Let cool to room temperature.

2 Meanwhile, in a medium pot, bring 3 cups water to a boil. Add lentils and return to a boil for 2 to 3 minutes. Reduce to a simmer and cook, covered, for 25 to 30 minutes until tender but not soft. Drain in a fine mesh colander and let cool to room temperature.

3 To assemble, in a large mixing bowl combine lentils, sweet potatoes, onion, celery, and feta. Mix well. Drizzle in honey, lemon juice, and remaining 1 tablespoon oil. Toss to combine. Taste and season with salt and pepper. Garnish with reserved celery leaves. Serve at room temperature.

Make it vegan

Use a nut-based vegan cheese alternative rather than feta.

Make it with meat

Include 4 slices bacon, crumbled, in lentil-feta mixture in step 3.

Nutrition per serving

Calories	480
Total Fat	19g
Saturated Fat	5g
Cholesterol	15mg
Sodium	1380mg
Total Carbohydrate	63g
Dietary Fiber	11g
Sugars	16g
Protein	17g

Pulse exchange

Substitute an equal amount dry **brown** or **green lentils** rather than beluga lentils.

CHICKPEA & CHERRY SALAD

This salad combines the flavors of summer in a single bowl. The tart sweetness of cherries mixes with the nuttiness of chickpeas to create an unusual side dish.

SERVES 4 · PREP 15 MINS

3 tbsp apple cider vinegar

1 tbsp olive oil

1 tsp honey

2 cups cooked chickpeas

1 cup dark-sweet cherries, pitted

2 tbsp chopped basil

1 ½oz (40 g) ricotta salata cheese, crumbled

Salt and pepper

1 To make dressing, in a small bowl whisk together vinegar, oil, and honey. Set aside.

2 In a large salad bowl, add chickpeas. Cut cherries in half and combine with chickpeas. Add basil and mix thoroughly. Drizzle dressing over mixture and toss to evenly coat.

3 Top with crumbled ricotta salata. Taste and season with salt and pepper and serve immediately.

Nutrition per serving

Calories	220
Total Fat	8g
Saturated Fat	2.5g
Cholesterol	10mg
Sodium	380mg
Total Carbohydrate	30g
Dietary Fiber	8g
Sugars	10g
Protein	9g

● Make it vegan

Omit ricotta salata and use ¼ cup capers for added brininess.

POTATO SALAD
WITH DIJON & LENTILS

Lentils elevate potato salad with extra texture, added bite, and lots of nutritious protein.

SERVES 6 · PREP 10 MINS · COOK 10 MINS

24oz (680g) small red potatoes, quartered

¼ cup plain Greek yogurt

2 tbsp mayonnaise

1 ½ tsp Dijon mustard

1 ½ tsp whole grain mustard

1 tsp red wine vinegar

1 cup cooked Beluga lentils

3 scallions, chopped

1 tbsp chopped chervil or parsley

Salt and pepper

1 Bring a large pot of water to a boil. Add potatoes and cook for 10 minutes, or until fork tender. Drain thoroughly.

2 Meanwhile, in a large mixing bowl, whisk together yogurt, mayonnaise, Dijon mustard, grain mustard, and red wine vinegar. Fold in cooked potatoes and Beluga lentils.

3 Sprinkle in scallions and chervil and stir to combine thoroughly. Taste and season with salt and pepper. Serve immediately or store in an airtight container for up to 2 days.

Nutrition per serving	
Calories	250
Total Fat	6g
Saturated Fat	0.5g
Cholesterol	<5g
Sodium	230g
Total Carbohydrate	42g
Dietary Fiber	8g
Sugars	3g
Protein	11g

● Make it with meat

For an extra punch of salt and crunch, stir in 5 ounces (140g) crispy bacon or pancetta, diced.

BLACK-EYED PEA FATTOUSH

Toasted bread, crisp vegetables, and lemony herbs add brightness to this hearty salad.

SERVES 8 · PREP 25 MINS · COOK 8 MINS

2 whole-wheat pitas, torn into 1-in (3cm) pieces

1 garlic clove, crushed

1 tsp sumac

4 tbsp olive oil

2 tbsp lemon juice

Salt and pepper

1 large cucumber, peeled, deseeded, and diced

½ cup grape tomatoes, halved

1 yellow or orange bell pepper, deseeded and diced

1 cup cooked black-eyed peas

⅓ cup chopped flat-leaf parsley

¼ cup chopped mint

1 Preheat the oven to 375°F (190°F). On a baking sheet, arrange pita in a single layer. Toast for 8 minutes, or until crispy and lightly golden brown. Remove from the oven and let cool.

2 To make dressing, in a small bowl, whisk together garlic, sumac, oil, and lemon juice. Taste and season with salt and pepper. Set aside.

3 In a large mixing bowl, combine cucumber, tomato, bell pepper, and black-eyed peas, and drizzle in dressing. Add parsley and mint and toss to combine. Add toasted pita and toss again. Season with salt and pepper. Serve immediately.

Nutrition per serving	
Calories	170
Total Fat	10g
Saturated Fat	1.5g
Cholesterol	0mg
Sodium	480mg
Total Carbohydrate	20g
Dietary Fiber	5g
Sugars	2g
Protein	5g

● Make it with meat

Add 1 pound (450g) grilled chicken or steak, chopped, along with pita in step 3.

CHICKPEA & KALE CAESAR SALAD

Chickpeas make two appearances in this Caesar salad. They're the creamy emulsifier in the garlicky dressing, and they're the crispy and nutritious alternative to croutons.

SERVES 6 · PREP 20 MINS · COOK 5 MINS

1 bunch kale

1 ½ cups cooked chickpeas

1 tbsp mayonnaise or plain Greek yogurt

2 tsp Dijon mustard

2 garlic cloves

Juice 2 medium lemons

1 cup olive oil

¼ cup freshly grated Parmesan cheese, optional

1 On a clean kitchen towel, arrange 1 cup cooked chickpeas in a single layer. Let air dry while you work.

2 Remove and discard tough ribs and stems from kale and chop leaves into bite-sized pieces. Rinse to remove grit and drain.

3 Meanwhile, to make dressing, in a blender combine the remaining ½ cup chickpeas, mayonnaise, Dijon mustard, garlic, and lemon juice. With the blender running, drizzle in ½ cup oil and blend until smooth. Set aside.

4 In a medium skillet, heat remaining ½ cup oil over medium-high heat. Once shimmering, carefully add dried chickpeas and fry for 3 to 4 minutes until golden brown and crispy. Remove and place on a plate lined with paper towel to absorb excess oil.

5 In a large mixing bowl, toss together kale and dressing, using your hands to massage and thoroughly coat kale. Transfer to serving plates and top with fried chickpeas. If using, top with grated Parmesan. Serve immediately.

Make it vegan

Replace mayonnaise with plain soy yogurt and replace Parmesan with nutritional yeast.

Make it with meat

For extra protein, top salad with grilled, sliced chicken breast.

Nutrition per serving

Calories	270
Total Fat	20g
Saturated Fat	3.5g
Cholesterol	<5mg
Sodium	125mg
Total Carbohydrate	17g
Dietary Fiber	4g
Sugars	2g
Protein	7g

Why not try...
For bright color, add ½ cup halved cherry or grape tomatoes.

LIMA BEAN PANZANELLA

Panzanella is a Tuscan bread salad that is quite popular in the warmer months. It's a great use for day-old bread and wonderful for parties and potlucks, as it can be served at room temperature.

SERVES 6 · PREP 25 MINS · COOK 15 MINS

1 small loaf sourdough bread
¼ cup red wine vinegar
1 tbsp Dijon mustard
½ cup olive oil
2 garlic cloves, minced
1 tsp chopped oregano
1 tsp chopped basil
1 cup halved cherry tomatoes
1 ½ cups cooked lima beans
1 English cucumber, diced
1 cup fresh yellow corn
  kernels
Salt and pepper

1 Preheat the oven to 325°F (170°C). Cut bread into ½-inch (1cm) cubes to make about 4 cups. On a baking sheet, arrange cubed bread into a single layer and bake for 15 minutes, or until toasted and lightly golden brown.

2 Meanwhile, to make dressing, in a small bowl, whisk together vinegar and Dijon mustard. While whisking, drizzle in oil and thoroughly combine. Stir in garlic, oregano, and basil. Set aside.

3 To assemble, in a large mixing bowl add tomatoes, lima beans, cucumber, and corn. Fold in toasted bread, then drizzle vinaigrette over mixture. Toss to coat. Taste and season with salt and pepper. Serve immediately.

Nutrition per serving

Calories	430
Total Fat	12g
Saturated Fat	2g
Cholesterol	0mg
Sodium	380mg
Total Carbohydrate	69g
Dietary Fiber	9g
Sugars	5g
Protein	14g

● **Make it with meat**

Add ¼ pound (115g) cooked shrimp when you assemble the salad.

PATTIES, TACOS, & SANDWICHES

MUNG BEAN BURGERS
WITH RED CURRY AIOLI

This textured veggie burger includes mung beans to give the patty great bite and a lovely green color.

MAKES 6 · PREP 25 MINS · COOK 25 MINS

1 shallot, finely minced

1 garlic cloves, finely minced

2 cups cooked mung beans

¼ tsp ground coriander

Pinch red pepper flakes

2 tbsp chopped cilantro

1 tbsp chopped mint

2 large eggs, beaten

⅓ cup panko breadcrumbs

Salt and pepper

½ cup plain Greek yogurt

½ tbsp red curry paste

6 hamburger buns or small pitas

1 Preheat the oven to 375°F (190°C). Line a baking sheet with parchment paper or spray with cooking spray. In a large mixing bowl, combine shallot, garlic, mung beans, coriander, red pepper flakes, cilantro, and mint. With a pastry cutter or the back of a fork, lightly mash mixture, allowing about half of mung beans to remain intact.

2 Add eggs and stir to mix thoroughly. Gently fold in breadcrumbs and season with salt and pepper.

3 With a measuring cup, portion out ½ cup mung bean mixture. Invert onto the baking sheet and lightly flatten to make a patty. Repeat to make 6 patties total. Bake patties for 10 minutes on each side, gently flipping in between.

4 Meanwhile, to make red curry aioli, in a small mixing bowl whisk together yogurt and red curry paste. Taste and season with salt and pepper.

5 To assemble, spread curry aioli on the inside, bottom piece of bun or pita and top with a patty. Repeat for remaining patties and serve immediately.

Make it vegan

Mix 2 tablespoons flax seeds with 6 tablespoons water to replace each egg. Instead of Greek yogurt, use plain coconut yogurt.

Nutrition per burger

Calories	360
Total Fat	17g
Saturated Fat	3g
Cholesterol	70mg
Sodium	400mg
Total Carbohydrate	37g
Dietary Fiber	5g
Sugars	5g
Protein	13g

Why not try…
For a double dose of legumes and texture, top your burger with alfalfa sprouts.

RED LENTIL & SWEET POTATO CROQUETTES

These croquettes are a lovely balance of sweet and savory. They make an excellent side dish or main course meal when served with a crisp green salad.

Make it vegan

Mix 2 tablespoons flax seeds with 6 tablespoons water to replace each egg.

MAKES 12 · PREP 10 MINS · COOK 1 HR 30 MINS

1 cup dry red lentils

1 large sweet potato, cubed

2 large eggs, separately beaten

½ tsp cinnamon

¼ tsp paprika

½ tsp ground cayenne pepper

Zest 1 orange

1 ½ cups panko breadcrumbs

Salt and pepper

1 cup vegetable oil

1 In a medium saucepan, cover lentils with about 2 inches (5cm) cold water. Cover and bring to a boil then reduce to a simmer and cook for 20 minutes, or until completely tender. Let sit in a mesh colander for at least 30 minutes, or until completely drained.

2 Meanwhile, bring a large stockpot full of water to a boil. Add sweet potatoes and cook, covered, for 20 minutes, or until fork tender. Let sit for at least 30 minutes, or until completely drained.

3 In a food processor, purée sweet potatoes until smooth. Transfer to a large mixing bowl and incorporate red lentils, 1 egg, cinnamon, paprika, cayenne, orange zest, and ½ cup breadcrumbs. Taste and season with salt and pepper. Refrigerate for 15 minutes, or until cool.

4 In a shallow baking dish, add remaining egg. In another shallow baking dish, add remaining 1 cup breadcrumbs. With your hands, form lentil mixture into 2-inch (5cm) cylindrical croquettes. Dredge in egg then gently roll in breadcrumbs until coated.

5 In a deep 12-inch (31cm) cast-iron skillet, heat oil over medium heat until shimmering. Working in batches, place croquettes into oil, rotating every 1 to 2 minutes until brown on all sides. Remove from oil and place on a plate lined with paper towel. Repeat with remaining croquettes. Serve immediately.

Nutrition per croquette

Calories	150
Total Fat	7g
Saturated Fat	5g
Cholesterol	30mg
Sodium	230mg
Total Carbohydrate	17g
Dietary Fiber	3g
Sugars	1g
Protein	6g

Pulse exchange

Use an equal amount **yellow lentils** rather than red lentils.

INDIAN POTATO & CHICKPEA PATTIES

The golden hue and warm Indian spices in these patties are reminiscent of masala dosa, a traditional potato-stuffed pancake. Serve these alongside chutney and raita.

MAKES 14 · PREP 25 MINS · COOK 1 HR

● **Make it vegan**

Instead of ghee, use any clear oil such as canola or vegetable.

4 ½ cups peeled and diced yukon gold potatoes (7–8 potatoes)

1 ½ cups cooked chickpeas

3 tbsp ghee

1 small red onion, finely diced

1 garlic clove, minced

1 ½ tsp garam masala

1 tsp ground ginger

¾ tsp ground coriander

½ cup cooked green peas

½ cup panko breadcrumbs

Salt and pepper

¼ cup chopped cilantro, for garnish

1 Bring a large stockpot full of water to a boil. Add potatoes and cook for 20 minutes, or until fork tender. Drain and let dry in colander for 15 minutes.

2 In a large mixing bowl, with a potato masher, roughly mash chickpeas. Add potatoes and mash again to combine.

3 In a medium nonstick skillet, heat 1 tablespoon ghee over medium-low heat. Add onion and cook for 2 to 3 minutes until soft. Add garlic and cook for an additional minute. Stir in garam masala, ginger, and coriander. Cook for an additional minute to warm spices.

4 In the mixing bowl, combine onion mixture with potato-chickpea mixture. Add remaining 2 tablespoons ghee and stir to combine. Stir in green peas and breadcrumbs. Mix thoroughly then taste and season with salt and pepper.

5 Portion out a ⅓ cup mixture and form into a patty with your hands. In a nonstick skillet, cook patty for 4 to 5 minutes on each side over medium-low heat until warmed through and lightly golden brown, adjusting heat as necessary to prevent burning. Work in batches to form and cook remaining mixture. Garnish with cilantro and serve immediately.

Nutrition per patty

Calories	100
Total Fat	4g
Saturated Fat	2g
Cholesterol	5g
Sodium	15g
Total Carbohydrate	13g
Dietary Fiber	3g
Sugars	2g
Protein	3g

Why not try... For heat, cook one small green chile, deseeded and minced, with garlic and onion.

BLACK-EYED PEA SLIDERS
WITH PICO DE GALLO

The pico de gallo on these sliders adds wonderful texture and moisture to the creamy black-eyed pea patties.

MAKES 8 · PREP 30 MINS · COOK 20 MINS

1 tbsp plus 1 tsp olive oil

1 small yellow onion, diced

1 garlic clove, minced

2 small jalapeños, deseeded and diced (about 3 tbsp)

½ tsp chipotle chili powder

2 ½ tsp ground cumin

2 ½ cups cooked black-eyed peas

2 large eggs, beaten

⅓ cup panko breadcrumbs

1 large tomato, deseeded and diced

1 small white onion, diced

¼ cup chopped cilantro

Juice 1 large lime

8 slider-sized hamburger buns

1 Preheat the oven to 300°F (150°C). In a large nonstick skillet, heat oil over medium-low heat until shimmering. Add yellow onion and cook for 2 minutes, or until soft. Add garlic and half of jalapeño. Cook for 2 minutes. Transfer mixture to a large mixing bowl and set aside. Set aside the skillet, leaving any residual oil.

2 Add chipotle chili powder, cumin, black-eyed peas, eggs, and breadcrumbs to vegetable mixture. With a potato masher, mix to combine and slightly break up black-eyed peas.

3 Return the skillet to the stove and heat over medium heat. Portion out ⅓ cup mixture and use your hands to form into a patty. Cook for 3 to 4 minutes on each side, pressing lightly with a spatula to sear. Transfer patty to a baking sheet. Repeat with remaining mixture to make 8 patties total, adding ½ teaspoon oil to the skillet between batches. Transfer the sheet to the oven and bake for 8 to 10 minutes until cooked through.

4 Meanwhilte, to make pico de gallo, in a small bowl, combine tomato, white onion, remaining jalapeño, cilantro, and lime. To assemble, place each patty on a slider bun and top with 1 tablespoon pico de gallo. Serve immediately.

● **Make it with meat**

To add smokiness, finely dice one slice bacon and cook along with garlic and jalapeño in step 1.

Nutrition per slider

Calories	230
Total Fat	6g
Saturated Fat	1g
Cholesterol	75mg
Sodium	290mg
Total Carbohydrate	34g
Dietary Fiber	5g
Sugars	4g
Protein	9g

Why not try...
Give these sliders more crunch by topping with shredded green or red cabbage.

PIGEON PEA PATTIES
WITH GUAVA SAUCE

These patties have all of the spice found in Jamaican jerk seasoning balanced with the sweet heat of the guava glaze.

MAKES 10 · PREP 30 MINS · COOK 45 MINS

½ cup guava jelly

2 tbsp red wine vinegar

¼ tsp red pepper flakes

2 tbsp vegetable oil or canola oil

1 small red onion, finely diced

1 Serrano chile, deseeded and minced

1 garlic clove, minced

½ tsp cinnamon

1 tsp ground cumin

¾ tsp ground nutmeg

1 ¼ tsp allspice

¼ tsp ground cayenne pepper

3 cups cooked pigeon peas

⅓ cup panko breadcrumbs

2 large eggs, beaten

3 tbsp chopped cilantro, to garnish

● Make it vegan

Instead of eggs, use ½ cup ripe avocado.

1 To make guava sauce, in a small saucepan, combine guava jelly, red wine vinegar, and red pepper flakes. Simmer over low heat for 8 to 10 minutes until jelly melts and mixture is syrupy. Remove from heat and keep warm on the stove.

2 Meanwhile, in a medium skillet, heat 1 tablespoon oil over medium-low heat. Add onion and cook for 2 to 3 minutes until soft. Then add Serrano chile and garlic and cook for an additional 1 to 2 minutes. Add cinnamon, cumin, nutmeg, allspice, cayenne, and 2 ½ cups pigeon peas. Stir to combine.

3 Transfer pigeon pea mixture to a food processor. Pulse until combined and slightly puréed. Then transfer to a large mixing bowl and add breadcrumbs, eggs, and remaining ½ cup whole pigeon peas. Fold together to combine.

4 Wipe out the medium skillet and return to the stove. Heat remaining 1 tablespoon oil over medium-low heat. Portion out ¼ cup pigeon pea mixture and place in the skillet. Slightly flattening with a spatula. Cook for 3 to 4 minutes on each side until golden brown.

5 Repeat with remaining mixture, adding oil to the skillet as necessary. Serve immediately with guava sauce.

Nutrition per patty

Calories	180
Total Fat	4g
Saturated Fat	0.5g
Cholesterol	35g
Sodium	20g
Total Carbohydrate	26g
Dietary Fiber	4g
Sugars	9g
Protein	5g

BLACK-EYED PEA & COLLARD GREEN TACOS

Black-eyed peas and greens are a classic pairing. Here, with some creamy goat cheese and a splash of hot sauce, they make a unique taco filling.

MAKES 12 · PREP 20 MINS · COOK 40 MINS

1 tbsp olive oil

1 small yellow onion, finely diced

1 garlic clove, minced

5 cups packed, rinsed, and roughly chopped collard greens

2 cups vegetable stock

½ tsp white wine vinegar

⅛ tsp ground cayenne pepper

2 cups cooked black-eyed peas

Salt and pepper

12 white or yellow corn tortillas

6oz (170g) goat cheese

Hot sauce, optional

1 In a medium Dutch oven or heavy-bottomed pot, heat oil over medium-low heat until shimmering. Add onion and cook for 2 to 3 minutes until soft. Add garlic and cook for an additional minute.

2 Stir in collard greens. Add stock, vinegar, and cayenne. Bring to a boil then reduce to a simmer and cook, covered, for 20 minutes, or until greens are tender. Add black-eyed peas and cook for an additional 10 minutes, or until beans are warmed through and most of liquid evaporates. Taste and season with salt and pepper.

3 Warm tortillas in a skillet or char lightly on the burner of a stove. To assemble, place one tortilla on a flat, clean work surface. Using a slotted spoon to drain away some of liquid, portion out ⅓ cup beans and greens mixture onto tortilla. Sprinkle with ½ ounce (14g) goat cheese and a few dashes hot sauce, if using. Roll taco, then repeat with remaining ingredients to make 12 tacos total. Serve immediately.

Make it vegan

Omit the goat cheese or use a non-dairy cheese alternative.

Make it with meat

Add 2 ½ ounces (70g) cooked smoked turkey or pork, chopped, along with greens in step 2.

Nutrition per taco

Calories	120
Total Fat	4.5g
Saturated Fat	2g
Cholesterol	5mg
Sodium	110mg
Total Carbohydrate	16g
Dietary Fiber	4g
Sugars	1g
Protein	6g

Why not try... Add a spoonful of your favorite salsa to each taco after goat cheese and hot sauce.

SPIRALIZED BEET & KIDNEY BEAN PATTIES

The hot pink color and texture from the beet is truly special. Serve as you would your favorite veggie burger or alongside grilled chicken or pork.

MAKES 8 · PREP 15 MINS · COOK 30 MINS

2 medium red beets, peeled

2 cups cooked kidney beans

1 tbsp chopped green onion

1 tbsp chopped cilantro

Pinch red pepper flakes

½ cup panko breadcrumbs

2 large eggs, beaten

Salt and pepper

1 Preheat the oven to 325°F (170°C). Line a baking sheet with parchment paper.

2 Adjust a spiralizer to the medium blade and spiralize beets. (This should yield about 3 cups.) With kitchen shears, cut strands into about 1-inch (3cm) pieces.

3 In a large mixing bowl, gently mash kidney beans with a fork or pastry cutter so some beans remain intact. Fold in spiralized beets, green onion, cilantro, red pepper flakes, breadcrumbs, and eggs. Season with salt and pepper to taste.

4 Heat a large nonstick skillet over medium heat. Form beet mixture into 8 equal patties. Place patties in the skillet and cook for 3 to 4 minutes on each side until brown and holding together. Arrange on the baking sheet.

5 Bake patties for 8 to 10 minutes until cooked through. Serve immediately.

● **Make it vegan**

Replace eggs with an extra ½ cup cooked kidney beans and 2 tablespoons water, puréed in a food processor, and add to mixture in step 3.

Nutrition per patty

Calories	100
Total Fat	1.5g
Saturated Fat	0g
Cholesterol	45mg
Sodium	330mg
Total Carbohydrate	16g
Dietary Fiber	4g
Sugars	2g
Protein	6g

Pulse exchange

Use an equal amount **pinto beans** instead of kidney beans.

RAINBOW LENTIL MEATBALLS
WITH ARRABIATTA SAUCE

Lentil meatballs and spicy tomato sauce are a healthy alternative to the comfort food classic, loaded with protein and fiber. Serve with pasta or bread and Parmesan cheese.

MAKES 18 · PREP 15 MINS · COOK 40 MINS

1 ½ cups cooked red lentils, thoroughly drained

⅔ cup cooked brown lentils, thoroughly drained

1 large egg, lightly beaten

½ cup panko breadcrumbs

½ tsp garlic powder

1 tsp dry oregano

Zest 1 large lemon

¼ tsp ground cayenne pepper

2 tbsp olive oil

1 small yellow onion, minced

28oz (800g) can crushed tomatoes

1 tbsp red pepper flakes

Salt and pepper

1 Preheat the oven to 350°F (180°C). Spray a baking sheet with cooking spray. In a large mixing bowl, combine red lentils, brown lentils, egg, breadcrumbs, garlic powder, oregano, lemon zest, and cayenne.

2 With your hands, form approximately 1 tablespoon lentil mixture into a meatball and place on the baking sheet. Repeat with remaining mixture. Bake for 25 minutes, rotating meatballs halfway through.

3 Meanwhile, to make arrabiatta sauce, in a saucepan warm oil over medium-low heat. Add onion and cook for 2 minutes, or until soft. Add crushed tomatoes and red pepper flakes. Simmer over low heat for 15 minutes, or until sauce is warmed through. Taste and season with salt and pepper.

4 Place meatballs on serving plates, top with arrabiatta sauce, and serve immediately.

Nutrition per meatball

Calories	70
Total Fat	2g
Saturated Fat	0g
Cholesterol	0mg
Sodium	115mg
Total Carbohydrate	9g
Dietary Fiber	2g
Sugars	2g
Protein	3g

●**Make it with meat**

Add ½ pound (225g) ground beef or crumbled Italian sausage along with onion in step 3.

YELLOW LENTIL & QUINOA CAKES

These little cakes come together quickly and make a great lunch alongside a salad.

MAKES 10 · PREP 10 MINS · COOK 45 MINS

⅔ cup cooked yellow lentils

Dash garlic powder

3 green onions, diced

2 tbsp chopped basil

2 tbsp chopped oregano

4 large eggs, beaten

1 cup panko breadcrumbs

4 cups cooked quinoa

1 tbsp olive oil

1 In a large mixing bowl, combine yellow lentils, garlic powder, green onions, basil, oregano, eggs, and breadcrumbs. Fold quinoa into lentil mixture and mix thoroughly.

2 Onto a damp plate, portion out ¼ cup lentil-quinoa mixture and gently shape into a small, flattened patty. Repeat to make 10 patties total and let sit for 5 minutes.

3 Meanwhile, in a medium nonstick skillet, heat oil over medium heat. Place patties in the skillet. Cook for 2 to 3 minutes on each side until golden and holding together. Serve immediately.

Nutrition per patty

Calories	170
Total Fat	5g
Saturated Fat	1g
Cholesterol	75mg
Sodium	45mg
Total Carbohydrate	23g
Dietary Fiber	4g
Sugars	1g
Protein	7g

● **Make it vegan**

Replace each egg with 3 tablespoons mashed potatoes.

BEAN FLAUTAS
WITH AVOCADO CREMA

Meaty Scarlet Runner beans and cheese fill these baked flautas, Spanish for *flute*.

MAKES 16 · PREP 20 MINS · COOK 10 MINS

1 cup sour cream

1 medium avocado, halved and pitted

Juice 1 lime

1 cup cooked Scarlet Runner beans

1 cup grated sharp Cheddar cheese

4oz (110g) goat cheese

½ cup chopped green onion

½ cup fresh corn kernels

⅓ cup chopped cilantro

1 tbsp ground cumin

1 tsp cayenne pepper

Salt

16 small flour tortillas

1 Preheat the oven to 400°F (200°C). Set up a mesh cooling rack on a rimmed baking sheet. To make crema, in a food processor or blender, combine sour cream, avocado, and lime juice until smooth. Refrigerate in a small bowl.

2 In a large mixing bowl, lightly mash Scarlet Runner with a potato masher. Incorporate Cheddar, goat cheese, green onion, corn, cilantro, cumin, and cayenne. Taste and season with salt.

3 To assemble, at one edge of tortilla, place 2 tablespoons filling and tightly roll, leaving ends open. Place seam-side down on the wire rack. Repeat to make 16 flautas total. Bake for 20 minutes, or until edges are lightly brown. Serve immediately with crema on the side.

Nutrition per flauta

Calories	210
Total Fat	8g
Saturated Fat	4g
Cholesterol	10mg
Sodium	440mg
Total Carbohydrate	25g
Dietary Fiber	3g
Sugars	1g
Protein	10g

● **Make it with meat**

Add 5 ounces (140g) cooked, shredded chicken or beef to filling when you add cheese. This yields at least 20 flautas.

HARISSA RED LENTIL MEATBALLS

These spicy lentil meatballs are an all-purpose vegetarian meal. Serve along with pasta, your choice of sauce, or even tucked into a pita.

MAKES 18 · PREP 30 MINS · COOK 35 MINS

1 medium yellow squash
3 tbsp olive oil
1 small yellow onion, diced
1 garlic clove, minced
2 ½ cups cooked red lentils
¾ cup panko breadcrumbs
1 ½ tbsp all-purpose flour
1 ½ tbsp harissa paste
1 ½ tsp tomato paste
1 tsp soy sauce
Zest 1 lemon
1 tbsp chopped cilantro
Salt and pepper

1 With the wide side of a box grater, grate squash into a rimmed pie pan or plate. Sprinkle salt and let rest in a fine mesh colander for 20 minutes. Press any remaining water out with your hands.

2 In a large skillet, warm 1 tablespoon oil over medium-low heat. Add onion and cook for 2 to 3 minutes until soft. Add garlic and cook for an additional minute. Add squash and cook for 3 to 4 minutes. Drain any remaining liquid from the skillet and transfer squash to a large mixing bowl. Wipe out the skillet and return to the stove.

3 To squash mixture, add red lentils, breadcrumbs, flour, harissa paste, tomato paste, soy sauce, lemon zest, and cilantro. Taste and season with salt and pepper.

4 In the skillet, heat remaining 2 tablespoons oil over medium heat. With your hands, form a heaping tablespoon squash mixture into a small ball and carefully place in the skillet. Working in batches, cook meatballs for 2 to 3 minutes on each side until lightly browned on all sides. Repeat with remaining mixture. Serve immediately.

Make it vegan

Substitute liquid aminos or coconut aminos rather than soy sauce.

Nutrition per meatball

Calories	70
Total Fat	2.5g
Saturated Fat	0g
Cholesterol	0mg
Sodium	170mg
Total Carbohydrate	9g
Dietary Fiber	2g
Sugars	1g
Protein	3g

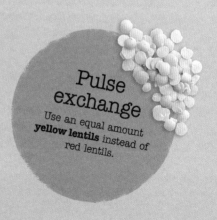

Pulse exchange

Use an equal amount **yellow lentils** instead of red lentils.

LENTIL PATE BANH MI

Creamy lentils replace traditional pate in this version of the Vietnamese sandwich. Don't skip the sprouted lentils—the texture of these and the crisp vegetables are delightful.

MAKES 4 · PREP 40 MINS · COOK 10 MINS, PLUS 1 HR TO CHILL

1 cup cooked green lentils

½ cup roughly chopped walnuts

1 tbsp miso paste

1 tsp soy sauce or liquid aminos

2 tsp apple cider vinegar

1 ½ tbsp olive oil

Salt and pepper

½ cup shredded carrot, julienned

½ cup grated daikon, julienned

⅓ cup rice wine vinegar

Pinch granulated sugar

½ cup sprouted brown lentils

1 long, thin French baguette

⅓ cup mayonnaise

1 small cucumber, peeled and cut into long strips

2 small jalapeños, thinly sliced

2 cups cilantro sprigs

1 To make lentil pate, in a food processor, combine green lentils, walnuts, miso paste, soy sauce, and apple cider wine vinegar. Blend on low and drizzle in oil until smooth. Taste and season with salt and pepper. Transfer to a small bowl and cover with plastic wrap, pressing the plastic onto top of lentil pate. Refrigerate for 1 hour.

2 In another small bowl, mix together carrot, daikon, rice wine vinegar, sugar, and sprouted lentils. Toss to coat thoroughly then refrigerate, covered, for at least 1 hour.

3 Preheat the oven to 350°F (180°C). Horizontally slice through baguette, leaving the side intact so bread is hinged. Then vertically cut fully through baguette to make 4 equal sections. Place 4 sections on a rimmed baking sheet and toast for 5 minutes, or until crispy but not hard. Let cool.

4 To assemble sandwiches, gently open hinged piece of baguettes. Spread equal amounts mayonnaise on inside, top pieces. Spread equal amounts lentil pate on inside, bottom pieces. Top lentil pate with equal amounts pickled carrot mixture, cucumber, jalapeños, and cilantro. Serve sandwiches immediately.

Make it vegan

Use an egg-free vegan mayonnaise rather than regular mayonnaise.

Make it with meat

Add 1 ounce (25g) sliced, roasted pork on top of lentil pate in each.

Why not try...

To make the banh mi heartier, add 1 ounce (25g) sliced and grilled tofu to each sandwich.

Nutrition per sandwich

Calories	440
Total Fat	24g
Saturated Fat	6g
Cholesterol	15mg
Sodium	760mg
Total Carbohydrate	46g
Dietary Fiber	8g
Sugars	10g
Protein	10g

PINTO BEAN & SPIRALIZED SWEET POTATO QUESADILLA

This quesadilla—a pressed, cheesy Mexican snack—is a great combination of heat from the jalapeño and sweetness from the potato. Spiralizing the sweet potato adds great texture to the dish.

MAKES 4 · PREP 20 MINS · COOK 40 MINS

1 small sweet potato, peeled

2 tbsp vegetable oil

1 jalapeño, deseeded and diced

4 large flour tortillas

2 cups finely shredded sharp Cheddar cheese

1 ⅓ cups cooked pinto or borlotti beans

½ cup chopped green onion

½ cup chopped cilantro

Sour cream, to serve

1 With the medium blade of a spiralizer, spiralize sweet potato.

2 In a medium skillet, heat oil over medium-low heat until shimmering. Add jalapeño and cook for 3 minutes, or until tender but not brown. Add spiralized sweet potato and cook for 7 minutes, or until tender but still al dente.

3 To assemble quesadilla, place tortilla on a clean, flat surface. Sprinkle ¼ cup Cheddar on lower half of tortilla. Top Cheddar with ⅓ cup pinto beans and ⅓ cup sweet potato mixture. Add 2 tablespoons onion and 2 tablespoons cilantro. Top with an additional ¼ cup Cheddar. Fold over top of tortilla to create a semi-circle. Repeat to make 4 quesadillas total.

4 Heat a nonstick skillet over medium heat. Add one quesadilla and cook for 4 minutes. Carefully flip, cover, and cook for an additional 4 minutes, or until tortilla is golden and Cheddar is melted. Repeat for remaining 3 quesadillas.

5 Cut each quesadilla into 4 sections. Serve immediately with sour cream on side.

Nutrition per quesadilla

Calories	640
Total Fat	33g
Saturated Fat	17g
Cholesterol	75mg
Sodium	840mg
Total Carbohydrate	61g
Dietary Fiber	9g
Sugars	4g
Protein	26g

● **Make it with meat**

Layer 1 ounce (25g) cooked, shredded chicken or pork on top of sweet potato in step 3.

SPICED LENTIL TACOS
WITH GRILLED PINEAPPLE SALSA

Grilling the pineapple in this salsa enhances its already intense sweetness and balances the heat from the jalapeño.

MAKES 8 · PREP 20 MINS ·COOK 45 MINS

1 cup dry brown lentils

2 ½ cups vegetable stock

1 bay leaf

Dash garlic powder

¼ tsp ground ginger

½ tsp allspice

1 ½ tsp ground cumin

12oz (340g) fresh pineapple slices

1 small jalapeño, deseeded and finely diced

1 small white onion, diced

½ cup chopped cilantro

Juice 1 lime

Salt and pepper

8 small corn tortillas

1 In a medium pot, combine lentils, stock, bay leaf, garlic powder, ground ginger, allspice, and cumin. Bring to a boil then reduce to a simmer. Cook over medium-low heat for 30 to 35 minutes until lentils are tender and most of stock has been absorbed, adding water as needed. Remove bay leaf and let sit, covered.

2 Meanwhile, heat a grill or grill pan over medium-high heat. Grill pineapple slices for 2 to 3 minutes on each side until caramelized. Remove from heat and let cool.

3 To make salsa, dice pineapple and combine in a small mixing bowl with jalapeño, onion, cilantro, and lime juice. Taste and season with salt and pepper.

4 To assemble each taco, place ¼ cup lentils onto tortilla, then top with 2 tablespoons salsa. Repeat to make 8 tacos. Roll tacos and serve immediately.

● **Make it with meat**

Incorporate 2 ½ ounces (70g) cooked, shredded, smoked pork or turkey to lentil mixture after removing bay leaf.

Nutrition per taco

Calories	170
Total Fat	1g
Saturated Fat	0g
Cholesterol	0mg
Sodium	55mg
Total Carbohydrate	33g
Dietary Fiber	10g
Sugars	5g
Protein	8g

Pulse exchange

Use an equal amount **Le Puy lentils** in place of brown lentils.

CRISPY AVOCADO & CHICKPEA TACOS

The crispy exterior of the avocado is a great contrast to the creamy interior. The resulting tacos are crispy, creamy, juicy, and delicious.

MAKES 4 · PREP 25 MINS · COOK 1 HR

2 cups soaked chickpeas

3 cups vegetable stock

1 tsp garlic powder

1 tbsp ground cumin

1 tbsp ancho chili powder

1 large egg, beaten

1 cup panko breadcrumbs

1 tsp chipotle chili powder

1 large ripe avocado

½ cup plain Greek yogurt

Zest and juice 1 large lime

4 large flour tortillas

1 cup finely shredded red cabbage

Salt and pepper

1 In a medium pot, combine chickpeas, stock, and garlic powder. Bring to a boil then reduce to a simmer and cook over low heat for 1 hour, adding additional water as needed until chickpeas are tender. Remove from heat, drain any excess liquid, and return to the pot. Stir in cumin and ancho chili powder. Let sit, covered.

2 Meanwhile, preheat the oven to 350°F (180°C). To prepare the breading station, arrange two small bowls in your workspace. Fill one with egg. In the second, combine breadcrumbs and chipotle chili powder. Set up a cooling rack on a rimmed baking sheet.

3 Halve avocado and remove pit. With skin on, cut each half into 4 wedges, making 8 slices. With a flexible spoon or knife, carefully remove flesh. Dip each slice into egg and then coat in breadcrumb mixture, shaking off excess at each step. Place slices on the cooling rack. Bake for 10 to 12 minutes, until crispy and lightly golden.

4 In a small bowl, whisk together yogurt and lime zest and juice. Taste and season with salt and pepper. To prepare each taco, spread 2 tablespoons yogurt on the bottom, then add ¼ cup chickpeas, 2 slices avocado, and ¼ cup cabbage. Roll and serve immediately.

● Make it vegan

Use 2 ½ tablespoons soy milk and 1 tablespoon ground flaxseed instead of egg. Replace Greek yogurt with soy yogurt.

Nutrition per taco

Calories	480
Total Fat	14g
Saturated Fat	2.5g
Cholesterol	50mg
Sodium	510mg
Total Carbohydrate	68g
Dietary Fiber	14g
Sugars	11g
Protein	19g

Pulse exchange Substitute an equal amount soaked **black beans** rather than chickpeas.

SCARLET RUNNER PATTIES
WITH AVOCADO SALAD

Scarlet Runner beans have a rich, meaty texture, making them perfect for veggie patties. The creamy avocado and brightness from the lime and cilantro balance the richness of the beans.

MAKES 8 · PREP 25 MINS · COOK 15 MINS

1 small yellow onion, finely diced

2 tbsp olive oil

3 cups cooked Scarlet Runner beans

1 tsp ground cumin

½ tsp smoked paprika

¼ tsp ground cayenne pepper

1 tsp all-purpose flour

Salt and pepper

1 large avocado, cubed

1 large red tomato, deseeded and diced

1 small white onion, diced

1 small jalapeño, deseeded and diced

2 tbsp chopped cilantro

Juice 1 large lime

1 Heat a medium nonstick skillet over medium-low heat. Add oil and heat until warm. Add yellow onion and cook for 2 to 3 minutes until soft but not brown. Add garlic and cook for an additional 1 to 2 minutes until soft. Remove from heat and let cool for 5 minutes.

2 In a food processor, combine 2 ½ cups Scarlet Runner and mixture from the skillet in step 1. Pulse until mashed but not puréed. Transfer to a large mixing bowl and stir in cumin, paprika, cayenne, flour, and remaining ½ cup whole Scarlet Runner. Taste and season with salt and pepper. Refrigerate for 15 minutes.

3 Meanwhile, to make salad, in a small mixing bowl combine avocado, tomato, white onion, jalapeño, cilantro, and lime juice. Taste and season with salt. Cover tightly and refrigerate until patties are cooked.

4 Heat a medium skillet over medium heat. Coat with cooking spray. Portion out ⅓ cup bean mixture and form into a patty with your hands. Place in the skillet and cook for 4 to 5 minutes per side until golden brown and holding shape. Repeat with remaining bean mixture. Top with avocado salad and serve immediately.

Nutrition per patty

Calories	170
Total Fat	8g
Saturated Fat	1.5g
Cholesterol	0mg
Sodium	280mg
Total Carbohydrate	21g
Dietary Fiber	8g
Sugars	4g
Protein	8g

Pulse exchange

Instead of Scarlet Runner beans, use 4 cups **kidney beans**—reserving 1 cup from the food processor in step 1.

GREEK WHITE BEAN TACOS

This twist on the traditional taco features ingredients typically found in a Greek salad. Romaine lettuce and cucumber add freshness and crunch to the creamy white beans and feta.

MAKES 8 · PREP 25 MINS · COOK 1 HR

2 tbsp olive oil

1 garlic clove, crushed

2 cups cooked navy beans

Zest and juice 1 large lemon

¼ cup vegetable stock

1 tbsp chopped oregano

Salt and pepper

½ cup plain Greek yogurt

8 small corn or flour tortillas

2 ½ cups shredded Romaine lettuce

2 cups diced Roma tomatoes

1 cup diced English cucumber

4oz (110g) crumbled feta cheese

1 In a small Dutch oven or pot, heat oil over medium-low heat. Add garlic and cook for 1 to 2 minutes until soft but not brown. Incorporate navy beans, lemon zest and juice, and stock.

2 Bring to a simmer then reduce heat to low and cook, covered, for 5 to 6 minutes until stock has been absorbed. Stir in oregano. Taste and season with salt and pepper.

3 To assemble, spread 1 tablespoon yogurt on a tortilla. Add ½ cup navy bean mixture. Top with about ⅓ cup Romaine, ¼ cup tomato, and 2 tablespoons cucumber. Sprinkle ½ ounce (14g) feta on top. Repeat with remaining tortillas, fold, and serve immediately.

Nutrition per taco

Calories	210
Total Fat	8g
Saturated Fat	3g
Cholesterol	15mg
Sodium	190mg
Total Carbohydrate	28g
Dietary Fiber	7g
Sugars	3g
Protein	11g

● Make it with meat

Add 2 ½ ounces (70g) cooked, chopped shrimp or chicken along with beans in step 1.

ZUCCHINI & LIMA BEAN FRITTERS

These fritters are light and refreshing, thanks to the lovely green color and burst of lemon zest. Serve as a side dish to grilled meats or top them with a poached egg and watercress.

MAKES 12 · PREP 20 MINS · COOK 30 MINS

4 medium zucchini

1 tbsp salt

1 ½ cups cooked lima beans

¼ tsp ground cayenne pepper

2 tsp chopped basil

Zest 1 large lemon

2 large eggs, beaten

¾ cup panko breadcrumbs

Salt and pepper

1 tbsp olive oil

1 With the wide side of a box grater, grate zucchini. Sprinkle with salt and place in a piece of cheesecloth or thin kitchen towel. Squeeze to remove as much water as possible and set aside.

2 In a food processor, combine lima beans, cayenne, basil, lemon zest, and egg. Blend on low for 30 to 45 seconds until smooth. Transfer to a large mixing bowl and add zucchini and breadcrumbs. Season with salt and pepper to taste. Stir to combine thoroughly.

3 In a nonstick skillet, heat oil over medium heat. Portion out 4 tablespoons lima bean–zucchini mixture, gently form into a ball, and place in the skillet. With a spatula, lightly press down to form a patty. Working in batches, form remaining patties and cook for 2 to 3 minutes on each side until lightly browned. Serve immediately.

● Make it vegan

Use 6 tablespoons water and 2 tablespoons ground flax seeds, combined, to replace egg.

Nutrition per patty

Calories	60
Total Fat	1g
Saturated Fat	0g
Cholesterol	30mg
Sodium	220mg
Total Carbohydrate	10g
Dietary Fiber	2g
Sugars	2g
Protein	4g

Why not try...

Add additional herbs such as oregano or marjoram to fritter mixture, to taste.

BAKED FALAFEL
WITH PICKLED RED ONIONS & SAMBAL OELEK

This falafel is oven-baked instead of fried for a healthier spin on this classic Middle Eastern street food. Pickled onions and sambal oelek are the perfect tangy-sweet and spicy condiments.

MAKES 16 · PREP 30 MINS, PLUS 3 HRS TO CHILL · COOK 40 MINS

1 cup apple cider vinegar

½ cup red wine vinegar

2 tbsp granulated sugar

1 tsp salt

1 large red onion, thinly sliced

1 garlic clove

2 cups cooked chickpeas

½ tsp baking soda

½ tsp ground coriander

½ tsp ground cumin

Pinch red pepper flakes

1 bunch curly parsley, chopped

½ cup finely chopped cilantro

Zest and juice 1 lemon

¼ cup chickpea flour

1 tbsp olive oil

Salt and pepper

¼ cup sambal oelek

1 To make pickled red onions, in a medium saucepan, bring apple cider vinegar, red wine vinegar, sugar, and salt to a boil over medium heat. Stir until sugar and salt dissolve. Remove from heat. Add red onion and stir to combine. Let cool completely at room temperature, stirring occasionally. Pour into a glass jar and secure with a lid. Refrigerate for 3 hours or overnight.

2 Preheat the oven to 400°F (200°C). In a food processor, combine garlic, chickpeas, baking soda, coriander, cumin, red pepper flakes, parsley, cilantro, and lemon zest and juice. Pulse until combined but still crumbly.

3 Transfer chickpea mixture to a medium mixing bowl and fold in chickpea flour. Drizzle oil over mixture and stir once more to combine, until holding together. Season with salt and pepper to taste.

4 Portion out approximately 2 tablespoons chickpea mixture and roll into a ball with your hands. Place on a baking sheet and repeat with remaining mixture. With a spatula, slightly flatten each to form patties. Bake for 10 minutes, flip, and bake for an additional 10 minutes. Serve immediately with the pickled red onions and sambal oelek on side.

● **Make it with meat**

Add 8 ounces (225g) raw ground lamb along with olive oil in step 3.

Nutrition per patty

Calories	60
Total Fat	1.5g
Saturated Fat	0g
Cholesterol	0mg
Sodium	270mg
Total Carbohydrate	9g
Dietary Fiber	2g
Sugars	2g
Protein	2g

Why not try...
If you'd rather skip the heat, serve with tzatziki sauce instead of spicy sambal.

BRAISES
& CURRIES

CHICKPEA TIKKA MASALA
IN LETTUCE CUPS

Creamy and surprisingly mild, the curry flavor in this dish is a wonderful match for the slightly sweet butter lettuce and the textured chickpeas.

SERVES 6 · PREP 20 MINS · COOK 30 MINS

1 tbsp ghee

1 small yellow onion, diced

1 tbsp garam masala

½ tsp turmeric

1 small green chile, deseeded and minced

¼ tsp grated ginger

2½ cups cooked chickpeas

2 cups tomato purée

¼ cup plain Greek yogurt

Salt and pepper

12 leaves butter lettuce, washed and dried

¼ cup thinly sliced red onion

2 tbsp chopped cilantro

1 In a large skillet, heat ghee over medium-low heat until shimmering. Add yellow onion and cook for 2 minutes, or until soft. Add garam masala, turmeric, chile, and ginger. Cook for an additional minute to warm spices.

2 Stir in chickpeas, tomato purée, and yogurt. Bring to a boil then reduce heat to low and cook for 20 minutes, or until sauce and chickpeas are completely warmed through. Taste and season with salt and pepper. Remove from heat and let sit for 5 minutes.

3 To assemble, portion chickpea mixture evenly into each leaf. Garnish with red onion and cilantro and serve immediately.

Make it vegan

Replace ghee with canola oil and Greek yogurt with coconut milk yogurt.

Make it with meat

Add 4½ ounces (130g) cooked, chopped chicken breast along with chickpeas in step 2.

Nutrition per serving

Calories	100
Total Fat	2.5g
Saturated Fat	1g
Cholesterol	<5mg
Sodium	100mg
Total Carbohydrate	15g
Dietary Fiber	4g
Sugars	5g
Protein	5g

Why not try...

For texture and crunch, use Savoy or Napa cabbage in place of butter lettuce.

GREEN CURRY LENTILS & BROCCOLI

The crunch of broccoli complements the creamy curry sauce, and the lentils introduce another layer of texture to this Thai dish that's perfect over brown basmati or jasmine rice.

SERVES 8 · PREP 30 MINS · COOK 35 MINS

1 tbsp vegetable oil

1 shallot, minced

1 garlic clove, minced

1 tbsp green curry paste

14fl oz (400 ml) can coconut milk

½ tbsp soy sauce

1 kaffir lime leaf or 1 tbsp fresh lime juice

1 small red bell pepper, deseeded and julienned

3 cups broccoli florets

1 cup cooked green lentils

3.5oz (100g) shiitake mushrooms, sliced

⅔ cup chopped fresh green beans

1 tbsp finely chopped basil

Salt and pepper

1 In a large pot, warm oil over medium-low heat until shimmering. Add shallot and garlic and cook for 2 minutes, or until soft. Add curry paste and stir to combine. Cook for an additional minute.

2 Add coconut milk, soy sauce, and kaffir lime leaf or lime juice. Simmer for 10 minutes. Add red bell pepper and cook for an additional 10 minutes, or until pepper starts to become tender.

3 Fold in broccoli, lentils, mushrooms, green beans, and basil. Cook for an additional 5 to 10 minutes until green beans and broccoli are tender and mushrooms are cooked. Remove kaffir lime leaf, if using. Taste and season with salt and pepper. Serve immediately.

Nutrition per serving

Calories	150
Total Fat	11g
Saturated Fat	9g
Cholesterol	0mg
Sodium	200mg
Total Carbohydrate	11g
Dietary Fiber	4g
Sugars	3g
Protein	4g

●Make it with meat

Add ½ pound (225g) raw chicken breast, sliced, and cook with shallots and garlic in step 1.

TOMATO BRAISED WHITE BEANS
WITH GREEN OLIVE POLENTA

These bright, acidic stewed beans served atop creamy polenta are comforting and filling.

SERVES 8 · PREP 20 MINS · COOK 1 HR 40 MINS

1 tbsp olive oil

1 small yellow onion, diced

1 small carrot, diced

1 celery stalk, diced

1 garlic clove, minced

1 bay leaf

⅛ tsp red pepper flakes

1 rosemary sprig

2 cups soaked Great Northern beans

28oz (794g) can crushed tomatoes

3–3 ½ cups vegetable stock

4 cups whole milk

2 cups fine grind cornmeal

½ cup pitted green olives, chopped

Salt and pepper

1 In a large Dutch oven or heavy-bottomed pot, heat oil over medium-low heat. Add onion, carrot, and celery and cook for 2 to 3 minutes until soft. Add garlic and cook for an additional 1 to 2 minutes.

2 Add bay leaf, red pepper flakes, rosemary, Great Northern beans, crushed tomatoes, and 1 cup stock. Bring to a boil then reduce to a simmer over low heat, and cook, covered, for 1 hour, or until beans are tender all the way through, adding up to ½ cup stock as needed. Turn off heat and let sit, covered.

3 To make polenta, in a medium saucepan, bring remaining 2 cups stock and whole milk to a boil then reduce to a simmer over low heat. Gradually whisk in cornmeal and stir constantly for 5 to 6 minutes until mixture tightens up. Stir in olives and cook for an additional minute. Taste and season with salt and pepper.

4 Remove rosemary stem and bay leaf from bean mixture. Portion polenta into a bowl and top with bean mixture. Serve immediately.

Nutrition per serving

Calories	410
Total Fat	9g
Saturated Fat	3.5g
Cholesterol	15mg
Sodium	430mg
Total Carbohydrate	60g
Dietary Fiber	14g
Sugars	13g
Protein	18g

● Make it vegan

Replace whole milk with a non-dairy alternative such as almond milk.

● Make it with meat

Stir in ½ pound (225g) crumbled chorizo, cooked, once beans are tender.

Pulse exchange

Substitute an equal amount **flageolet beans** rather than Great Northern beans.

RED KIDNEY BEAN CURRY

Meaty kidney beans are simmered in a spicy onion-tomato sauce to create this simple curry, a comforting staple dish in many Indian households and often served with basmati rice.

SERVES 6 · PREP 25 MINS · COOK 25 MINS

2 tbsp vegetable oil

1 medium onion, diced

3 garlic cloves, finely minced

2 tsp grated ginger

1 small green or red chile, deseeded and minced

1 ½ cups crushed tomatoes

¼ tsp turmeric

1 tbsp ground coriander

1 tbsp ground cumin

1 ½ tsp garam masala

3 cups cooked kidney beans

½ cup vegetable stock

Salt and pepper

¼ cup chopped cilantro

1 In a heavy-bottomed pot or Dutch oven, heat oil over medium-high heat. Add onion and cook for 2 to 3 minutes until it begins to soften. Add garlic, ginger, and chile and cook for an additional 1 to 2 minutes.

2 Add crushed tomatoes, turmeric, coriander, cumin, and garam masala. Bring sauce mixture to a boil then reduce heat to low and cook, covered, for 7 to 8 minutes until sauce begins to thicken, stirring regularly.

3 Add kidney beans and stock. Cook for an additional 10 minutes, or until beans are heated through, stirring regularly. Taste and season with salt and pepper. Portion into a serving bowl, garnish with cilantro, and serve immediately.

● **Make it with meat**

Add ½ pound (225g) raw, cubed chicken breast to the pot before adding garlic in step 1.

Nutrition per serving

Calories	180
Total Fat	4g
Saturated Fat	3g
Cholesterol	0mg
Sodium	170mg
Total Carbohydrate	28g
Dietary Fiber	9g
Sugars	4g
Protein	9g

Pulse exchange

Use an equal amount **pinto beans** instead of kidney beans.

DAL BOLOGNESE

There are few delights more comforting than the flavors of a slow-cooked, classic Bolognese sauce, used here to create a warmly spiced lentil dal. This is delicious atop rice or polenta.

SERVES 8 · PREP 30 MINS · COOK 1 HR

2 tbsp olive oil

2 celery stalks, finely diced

1 small yellow onion, finely diced

2 carrots, peeled and finely diced

2 garlic cloves, minced

2 cups dry brown lentils

28oz (794g) can crushed tomatoes

2 tbsp tomato paste

4 cups vegetable stock

1 bay leaf

½ cup heavy cream

¼ tsp ground nutmeg

Salt and pepper

1 In a Dutch oven or heavy-bottomed pot, heat oil over medium-low heat until shimmering. Add celery, onion, and carrot, and cook for 10 minutes, or until tender. Add garlic and cook for another 3 to 4 minutes.

2 Add lentils, crushed tomatoes, tomato paste, stock, and bay leaf. Bring to a gentle boil then reduce heat to low and simmer, covered, for 35 minutes, or until lentils are tender and sauce thickens.

3 Add heavy cream and nutmeg. Stir to combine and cook for an additional 5 minutes. Taste and season with salt and pepper. Remove bay leaf and serve immediately.

Make it vegan

Substitute soy creamer or soy milk instead of heavy cream.

Make it with meat

Add ½ pound (225g) raw Italian sausage, ground beef, or turkey along with celery in step 1.

Nutrition per serving

Calories	290
Total Fat	10g
Saturated Fat	4g
Cholesterol	20mg
Sodium	180mg
Total Carbohydrate	39g
Dietary Fiber	17g
Sugars	7g
Protein	14g

Pulse exchange

Use an equal amount **green lentils** rather than brown lentils.

DAL MAKHANI

These buttery lentils are rich and spicy. Serve the creamy Indian recipe with warm naan to soak up the luscious sauce.

SERVES 4 · PREP 20 MINS · COOK 1 HR

2 tbsp ghee or vegetable oil

1 garlic clove, minced

1 ½ tsp grated ginger

1 small green chile, deseeded and minced

1 ¼ tsp turmeric

1 ¼ tsp ground coriander

1 ½ cups tomato purée

½ cup water

2 ½ cups cooked black gram

⅓ cup heavy cream

Salt

⅓ cup chopped cilantro

1 In a medium stockpot, warm ghee over medium-low heat until shimmering. Add garlic, ginger, and chile and cook for 2 to 3 minutes until soft. Stir in turmeric and coriander.

2 Stir in tomato purée, water, and black gram. Cook, uncovered, for 5 to 6 minutes until liquid reduces and thickens slightly.

3 Slowly stir in heavy cream. Simmer, uncovered, over low heat for an additional 10 minutes. Taste and season with salt. Garnish with cilantro and serve immediately.

Nutrition per serving	
Calories	430
Total Fat	20g
Saturated Fat	11g
Cholesterol	45mg
Sodium	200mg
Total Carbohydrate	49g
Dietary Fiber	10g
Sugars	8g
Protein	16g

● **Make it vegan**

Use an equal amount coconut milk instead of heavy cream.

WHITE BEAN COCONUT CURRY

This spicy curry is super creamy thanks to the smooth navy beans and the rich sauce.

SERVES 6 · PREP 25 MINS · COOK 35 MINS

1 tbsp coconut oil

1 small yellow onion, diced

1 orange or yellow bell pepper, diced

1 garlic clove, minced

1 tsp grated ginger

2 tbsp red curry paste

2 tbsp tomato paste

1 tsp ground coriander

½ tsp garam masala

¼ tsp turmeric

13 ½fl oz (400ml) can coconut milk

3 cups cooked navy beans

½ cup chopped cilantro

1 In a medium heavy-bottomed pot, heat oil over medium-low heat until shimmering. Add onion and bell pepper and cook for 2 minutes, or until soft. Add garlic and ginger and cook for 2 minutes.

2 Stir in red curry paste, tomato paste, coriander, garam masala, and turmeric. Cook for 1 minute to warm spices. Pour in coconut milk and stir to combine.

3 Add navy beans and bring to a boil. Reduce heat to low and simmer, covered, for 20 minutes, or until sauce thickens and beans are warmed through. Garnish with cilantro and serve immediately.

Nutrition per serving	
Calories	280
Total Fat	14g
Saturated Fat	11g
Cholesterol	0mg
Sodium	160mg
Total Carbohydrate	31g
Dietary Fiber	11g
Sugars	3g
Protein	9g

● **Make it with meat**

Sauté ½ pound (225g) peeled and deveined shrimp with butter and garlic and serve atop dish.

CAJUN BRAISED BLACK-EYED PEAS

Vinegar and spicy cayenne balance earthy black-eyed peas for Southern Creole flavor. Serve these brothy beans with cooked brown rice or quinoa to make a true cajun meal.

● Make it with meat

Add 2 ½ ounces (70g) cooked, cubed ham or smoked pork to braising liquid along with beans.

SERVES 4 · PREP 15 MINS · COOK 50 MINS

1 tbsp canola or vegetable oil

1 medium green bell pepper, finely diced

1 medium yellow onion, finely diced

1 celery stalk, finely diced

1 garlic clove, minced

5 thyme sprigs

1 bay leaf

2 ½ cups vegetable stock

2 cups soaked black-eyed peas

¾ tsp ground cayenne pepper

½ tsp paprika

1 tbsp white wine vinegar

Salt and pepper

1 In a medium Dutch oven or heavy-bottomed pot, heat oil over medium-low heat. Add bell pepper, onion, and celery. Cook for 3 to 4 minutes until soft. Add garlic and cook for an additional 1 to 2 minutes.

2 Add thyme, bay leaf, and stock. Bring to a boil then reduce heat and simmer for 5 minutes. Stir in black-eyed peas, cayenne, and paprika.

3 Bring to a boil then reduce heat to low and cook, covered, for 30 to 40 minutes until peas are tender. Add up to ½ cup additional stock or water as needed.

4 Stir in vinegar and taste and season with salt and pepper. Remove thyme stems and bay leaf. Serve immediately.

Nutrition per serving

Calories	270
Total Fat	5g
Saturated Fat	0g
Cholesterol	0mg
Sodium	780mg
Total Carbohydrate	41g
Dietary Fiber	11g
Sugars	5g
Protein	13g

Pulse exchange

Use 1 ½ cups soaked **pigeon peas** rather than black-eyed peas.

BRAISED LEEKS & LE PUY LENTILS

Simple to make yet sophisticated in flavor, braising leeks brings out their subtle sweetness and contrasts beautifully with the earthy flavor of French Le Puy lentils.

SERVES 6 · PREP 15 MINS · COOK 30 MINS

6 leeks

3 tbsp unsalted butter

1 tbsp dry vermouth

3 thyme sprigs

½ cup vegetable stock

1 cup cooked Le Puy or green lentils

Salt and pepper

2 tbsp chopped flat-leaf parsley

1 Carefully trim and remove root from leeks while keeping them intact. Cut off dark green tops and remove tough outer layers. Cut each leek in half lengthwise. Submerge in cold water for 5 minutes to remove any dirt from inside. Transfer to a colander and let drain.

2 In a 12-inch (30cm) skillet, melt butter over medium-low heat. Add vermouth. Place leeks cut-side down in the skillet and cook for 4 minutes.

3 Add thyme and stock. Bring to a gentle boil then reduce to a simmer. Cook, covered, for 10 to 15 minutes until leeks are fork tender.

4 Add lentils and cook for an additional 5 minutes. Taste and season with salt and pepper.

5 Remove thyme stems. With tongs, transfer leeks to a serving platter. Pour lentils and cooking liquid over leeks. Garnish with parsley and serve immediately.

Make it vegan

Replace unsalted butter with a vegan butter alternative.

Make it with meat

Instead of butter, render fat of 6 strips raw, chopped bacon, then proceed with vermouth in step 2, leaving bacon bits in the skillet.

Pulse exchange

Rather than lentils, use an equal amount **black gram** or **moth beans.**

Nutrition per serving

Calories	150
Total Fat	6g
Saturated Fat	3g
Cholesterol	15mg
Sodium	20mg
Total Carbohydrate	19g
Dietary Fiber	4g
Sugars	4g
Protein	4g

BRAISED LIMA & NAVY BEANS
WITH CHERMOULA

Originally from North Africa, chermoula is a tart, herby sauce. Its punchy flavors and bright color offer a tasty complement to creamy braised beans.

● Make it with meat

Stir in 1 ounce (25g) cooked, chopped, smoked pork when you add beans.

SERVES 6 · PREP 35 MINS · COOK 30 MINS

2 cups roughly chopped parsley

2 cups roughly chopped cilantro

5 garlic cloves

1 tbsp smoked paprika

1 ½ tsp ground cumin

2 tbsp cold water

2 tbsp lemon juice

¼ cup plus 1 tbsp olive oil

1 small yellow onion, diced

1 celery stalk, diced

1 large carrot, diced

1 bay leaf

4 thyme sprigs

2 ½ cups vegetable stock

2 cups cooked lima beans

2 cups cooked navy beans

Salt and pepper

1 To make chermoula, in a food processor, combine parsley, cilantro, 4 whole garlic cloves, paprika, cumin, water, and lemon juice. Process on low. With the processor running, drizzle in ¼ cup oil. Blend until smooth. Transfer contents to a small bowl and cover with plastic wrap, pressing to top of sauce so it does not oxidize. Refrigerate until ready to serve.

2 In a medium Dutch oven or heavy-bottomed pot, heat remaining 1 tablespoon oil over medium-low heat until warm. Add onion, celery, and carrot. Cook for 2 to 3 minutes until soft. Mince remaining garlic clove and add to vegetables. Cook for an additional minute.

3 Add bay leaf, thyme, stock, lima beans, and navy beans. Bring to a boil then reduce heat to low and cook, covered, for 20 minutes, or until liquid thickens and beans are warmed through. Taste and season with salt and pepper.

4 Remove bay leaf and thyme stems. Serve immediately with chermoula on the side.

Nutrition per serving

Calories	250
Total Fat	8g
Saturated Fat	1g
Cholesterol	0mg
Sodium	85mg
Total Carbohydrate	36g
Dietary Fiber	13g
Sugars	4g
Protein	11g

MOROCCAN SQUASH & PIGEON PEA TAGINE

This slow-cooked, warmly spiced squash stew receives its name from the earthenware pot in which it's traditionally cooked, but you can create the same depth of flavor even without a tagine.

SERVES 6 · PREP 45 MINS · COOK 40 MINS

1 tbsp coconut oil

1 medium yellow onion, chopped

1 carrot, diced

2 garlic cloves, minced

1 tsp grated ginger

1 tsp smoked paprika

1 cinnamon stick

¼ tsp allspice

½ tsp ground coriander

¼ tsp ground cardamom

2 tbsp tomato paste

2 cups vegetable stock

1 large acorn squash, peeled, deseeded, and cubed (yields about 4 cups)

2 cups cooked pigeon peas

Juice 1 large lemon

½ cup pitted and chopped dates

Salt and pepper

1 In a cast-iron tagine or large Dutch oven, heat coconut oil over medium-low heat. Add onion and carrot and cook for 2 to 3 minutes. Add garlic and ginger and cook, uncovered, for an additional 1 to 2 minutes.

2 Add paprika, cinnamon stick, allspice, coriander, and cardamom. Cook for 1 minute to warm spices. Add tomato paste and stock and stir to combine.

3 Stir in squash and simmer, covered, for 15 minutes. Add pigeon peas and cook for an additional 10 minutes, or until squash is tender and peas are warmed through. Stir in lemon juice and dates. Taste and season with salt and pepper. Remove cinnamon stick and serve immediately.

● **Make it with meat**

Brown 1 pound (450g) lamb shoulder, cubed, and add with acorn squash.

Nutrition per serving

Calories	210
Total Fat	2.5g
Saturated Fat	2g
Cholesterol	0mg
Sodium	260mg
Total Carbohydrate	41g
Dietary Fiber	8g
Sugars	22g
Protein	5g

Pulse exchange

For a traditional tagine, substitute an equal amount **chickpeas** instead of pigeon peas.

INDIAN SPICED SPINACH & LENTILS

Inspired by the Indian favorite *saag*, this recipe incorporates green lentils to add texture to the creamy spinach dish. Serve with warm garlic naan and rice for a complete meal.

SERVES 4 · PREP 15 MINS · COOK 30 MINS

1 ½ tsp cumin seeds

6 tbsp ghee

1 ½ tsp turmeric

½ tsp ground coriander

1 long green chile, deseeded and minced

2 garlic cloves, minced

24oz (680g) baby spinach

1 ½ cups cooked green lentils

¼ cup heavy cream

Salt and pepper

1 With a mortar and pestle, grind cumin seeds into a fine powder to release fragrance.

2 In a heavy-bottomed pot, heat ghee over medium-low heat until shimmering. Add cumin, turmeric, and coriander and cook for 1 minute. Add chile and cook for 3 minutes, or until it begins to soften. Add garlic and cook for an additional 2 minutes.

3 Add spinach. Stir to combine with spices and aromatics. Cook for 5 minutes, or until spinach begins to wilt.

4 Stir in green lentils and heavy cream. Simmer, partially covered, over low heat for 15 minutes, or until spinach is cooked and sauce thickens, stirring regularly.

5 Taste and season with salt and pepper. Serve immediately.

Make it vegan

Replace ghee with canola or vegetable oil and use non-dairy alternative to heavy cream.

Make it with meat

Add 4 ½ ounces (130g) cooked, chopped chicken breast along with the lentils in step 4.

Pulse exchange

Substitute 1 cup cooked **mung beans** for green lentils.

Nutrition per serving

Calories	420
Total Fat	11g
Saturated Fat	7g
Cholesterol	10mg
Sodium	135mg
Total Carbohydrate	57g
Dietary Fiber	32g
Sugars	<1g
Protein	24g

PIGEON PEA VINDALOO

Characteristic of vindaloo, the high heat level in this Indian curry perfectly balances with the warm spices, such as cinnamon and cardamom. Serve with rice or naan and some cooling yogurt.

SERVES 4 · PREP 25 MINS · COOK 35 MINS

1 ¼ tbsp ground cumin

1 tbsp ground coriander

¾ tsp turmeric

⅔ tsp ground cardamom

½ tbsp ground mustard

1 tbsp paprika

1 tbsp vegetable oil

1 small yellow onion, diced

3 garlic cloves, minced

¾ tbsp minced ginger

1 large Thai red chile, deseeded and minced

1 bay leaf

1 cinnamon stick

1 cup tomato purée

1 tbsp red wine vinegar

1 cup water

3 cups cooked pigeon peas

Salt and pepper

1 In a small bowl, combine cumin, coriander, turmeric, cardamom, mustard, and paprika and stir thoroughly to combine.

2 In a heavy-bottomed pan, heat oil over medium heat until shimmering. Add onion and cook for 3 to 4 minutes until it starts to become translucent.

3 Stir in garlic, ginger, and chile, and cook for an additional 2 minutes. Incorporate spice mixture, bay leaf, cinnamon stick, tomato purée, vinegar, and water, and bring to a boil. Reduce heat and simmer, covered, for 10 minutes.

4 Add pigeon peas and stir to combine. Bring to a boil then reduce to a simmer and cook, covered, for 20 minutes. Remove cinnamon stick and bay leaf. Taste and season with salt and pepper. Serve immediately.

Nutrition per serving

Calories	250
Total Fat	5g
Saturated Fat	3g
Cholesterol	0mg
Sodium	590mg
Total Carbohydrate	42g
Dietary Fiber	12g
Sugars	9g
Protein	11g

● **Make it with meat**

Brown 1 pound (450g) beef chuck, cubed, and add with tomato purée.

CURRIED SQUASH & MUNG BEAN DOPIAZA

The pronounced flavors of both caramelized onion and lightly sautéed onion combine with creamy coconut to create this *dopiaza*, a Hindi word meaning "two onions."

SERVES 6 · PREP 30 MINS · COOK 55 MINS

● **Make it with meat**

Reduce squash to 3 cups total and add 4 ½ ounces (130g) cooked, shredded or cubed chicken breast to the pan with squash.

4 cups peeled and cubed butternut squash

2 tbsp vegetable oil

2 medium yellow onions

2 garlic cloves, minced

1 tsp grated ginger

1 ½ tsp ground cumin

1 tsp ground coriander

2 ¼ tsp garam masala

1 tsp red pepper flakes

½ tsp turmeric

14fl oz (400ml) can coconut milk

3 Roma tomatoes, roughly chopped

1 cup vegetable stock

3 cups cooked mung beans

⅓ cup chopped cilantro

1 Preheat the oven to 375°F (190°C). Toss cubed squash with 1 tablespoon oil and spread in an even layer on a baking sheet. Roast for 15 to 25 minutes until tender, stirring occasionally.

2 Meanwhile, dice one onion and thinly slice other onion. Set aside in separate bowls.

3 In a large saucepan, heat remaining 1 tablespoon oil over medium-low heat until shimmering. To caramelize sliced onion, add to the saucepan and cook for 7 to 8 minutes until golden brown. Remove from the pan and set aside.

4 Add diced onion to the pan and cook for 2 to 3 minutes until soft. Add garlic and ginger and cook for an additional 1 to 2 minutes. Stir in cumin, coriander, garam masala, red pepper flakes, and turmeric, and cook for 1 minute to heat spices.

5 Pour in tomato purée, coconut milk, tomatoes, and stock. Bring to a boil then reduce to a simmer and cook for 5 minutes, or until ingredients are incorporated and tomatoes are tender. Remove from heat and let cool.

6 Pour tomato mixture from the saucepan into a blender and purée until smooth. Transfer sauce back to the pan. Warm over medium-low heat. Add roasted squash and mung beans. Simmer for 15 minutes, covered, or until sauce slightly thickens. Stir in caramelized sliced onions. Garnish with chopped cilantro and serve immediately.

Nutrition per serving

Calories	320
Total Fat	17g
Saturated Fat	14g
Cholesterol	0mg
Sodium	65mg
Total Carbohydrate	37g
Dietary Fiber	9g
Sugars	8g
Protein	10g

BRAISED WHITE BEANS
WITH SPINACH & POMEGRANATE

The creamy beans contrast with the cool, crunchy pomegranate seeds in this white bean braise. Make sure to add the seeds at the end to prevent your dish from turning pink!

SERVES 6 · PREP 20 MINS · COOK 30 MINS

1 tbsp olive oil

1 small yellow onion, diced

1 garlic clove, minced

3 thyme sprigs

¼ cup dry white wine

2 cups vegetable stock

3 cups cooked Great Northern beans

2 cups packed baby spinach

Salt and pepper

¼ cup finely grated Parmesan cheese

⅓ cup pomegranate seeds

1 In a medium Dutch oven or heavy-bottomed pot, heat oil over medium-low heat until shimmering. Add onion and cook for 2 to 3 minutes until soft. Add garlic and cook for an additional 1 to 2 minutes.

2 Stir in thyme, wine, and stock. Bring to a boil then reduce to a simmer. Add Great Northern beans and return to a boil. Then reduce heat and simmer again, covered, stirring occasionally, for 20 minutes, or until liquid slightly reduces and beans are heated through.

3 Remove the lid, stir in spinach, and cook over medium-low heat, uncovered, for 4 to 5 minutes. Taste and season with salt and pepper.

4 Remove from heat, remove thyme stems, and stir in Parmesan. Sprinkle pomegranate seeds on top and serve immediately.

● Make it vegan

Replace Parmesan with an equal amount nutritional yeast.

● Make it with meat

For a deeper flavor, add 1 ounce (25g) diced pancetta along with onion.

Nutrition per serving

Calories	180
Total Fat	4g
Saturated Fat	1g
Cholesterol	<5mg
Sodium	120mg
Total Carbohydrate	24g
Dietary Fiber	7g
Sugars	4g
Protein	10g

Pulse exchange

Rather than Great Northern beans, use an equal amount **flageolet beans.**

SWEET & SOUR CABBAGE
WITH BROWN LENTILS

This is an easy version of a German classic. Sugar, apple, and vinegar combine for a pleasantly smooth flavor that's even more delicious when re-heated the next day—so bring it for lunch the next day.

SERVES 4 · PREP 20 MINS · COOK 50 MINS

1 tbsp olive oil

1 shallot, minced

1 head red cabbage, core removed and shredded

1 small Granny Smith apple, peeled and thinly sliced

¼ tsp fennel seed

3 tbsp light brown sugar

½ cup apple cider vinegar

1 cup cooked brown lentils

1 In a Dutch oven or heavy-bottomed pot, warm oil over medium heat. Add shallot and cook for 3 minutes, or until soft but not brown. Add cabbage and apple and stir to combine.

2 Add fennel seed, brown sugar, and vinegar. Bring to a boil then reduce heat to low and simmer, covered, for 25 minutes.

3 Add lentils, stir thoroughly, and re-cover. Cook for an additional 20 minutes, or until cabbage is tender and lentils are warmed through. Serve immediately.

Nutrition per serving

Calories	210
Total Fat	4g
Saturated Fat	0g
Cholesterol	0mg
Sodium	60mg
Total Carbohydrate	41g
Dietary Fiber	9g
Sugars	23g
Protein	8g

● **Make it with meat**

Add 2 slices raw, chopped bacon and cook alongside shallot in step 1.

BRAISED CHICKPEAS
WITH PRESERVED LEMON

A North African condiment, these lemon slices packed in a brine of salt and water add a fragrant touch to this simple chickpea and chard braise.

● Make it
with meat

Finely dice 2 ounces (55g) pancetta and cook alongside onion in step 1.

SERVES 6 · PREP 15 MINS · COOK 35 MINS

1 tbsp olive oil

1 small yellow onion, chopped

1 garlic clove, minced

3 cups cooked chickpeas

1lb (450g) Swiss chard (chopped leaves and stems)

½ cup vegetable stock

½ cup chopped green olives

½ tbsp minced preserved lemon, or zest and juice 1 medium lemon

Salt and pepper

1 In a large Dutch oven, warm oil over medium heat until shimmering. Add onion and cook for 2 minutes, or until soft. Add garlic and cook for an additional minute.

2 Add chickpeas and Swiss chard and stir to combine. Add stock and cook, covered, for 15 minutes, or until chard begins to wilt.

3 Stir in olives and preserved lemon. Cook, covered, for an additional 10 minutes. Taste and season with salt and pepper. Serve immediately.

Pulse exchange
Use an equal amount **Great Northern beans** instead of chickpeas.

Nutrition per serving

Calories	190
Total Fat	6g
Saturated Fat	1g
Cholesterol	0mg
Sodium	530mg
Total Carbohydrate	29g
Dietary Fiber	8g
Sugars	7g
Protein	9g

LENTIL & TOMATO BRAISED GREEN BEANS

The secret of this dish is in the yellow tomatoes—they have an acidity that brightens the entire recipe. You'll be surprised at the depth of flavor achieved from such a simple braise.

● **Make it with meat**
For a salty, smoky flavor, cook 1 ounce (25g) pancetta along with onion.

SERVES 6 · PREP 15 MINS · COOK 1 HR 10 MINS, PLUS 5 MINS TO COOL

- ¾lb (365g) green beans
- 1 tbsp olive oil
- 1 small yellow onion, finely diced
- 1 garlic clove, minced
- 1 dry pint golden cherry tomatoes, halved
- ¼ cup dry white wine
- 1 ½ cups vegetable stock
- Pinch red pepper flakes
- ⅔ cup cooked brown lentils
- Salt and pepper

1 Remove ends from green beans. Rinse and let drain. In a medium Dutch oven or heavy-bottomed pot, heat oil over medium-low heat. Add onion and cook for 2 to 3 minutes until soft. Add garlic and cook for an additional 1 to 2 minutes.

2 Add cherry tomatoes and dry white wine. Stir to combine and cook, covered, for 5 minutes. Add stock and red pepper flakes. Bring to a boil then reduce to a simmer and cook, covered, for 15 minutes, stirring occasionally.

3 Add green beans. Return to a simmer and cook, covered, for 10 minutes. Add brown lentils and cook, covered, for 30 minutes, or until green beans are tender and liquid thickens. Taste and season with salt and pepper.

4 Remove from heat and let sit, covered, for 5 to 10 minutes to let any remaining liquid thicken. Serve immediately.

Nutrition per serving

Calories	140
Total Fat	2.5g
Saturated Fat	0g
Cholesterol	0mg
Sodium	40mg
Total Carbohydrate	21g
Dietary Fiber	9g
Sugars	5g
Protein	7g

Pulse exchange
Substitute an equal amount cooked **Le Puy** or **green lentils** instead of brown lentils.

FRIJOLES BORRACHOS

This Mexican recipe translates to "drunken beans"—a savory, soupy, and scrumptious all-purpose dish.

SERVES 8 · PREP 20 MINS · COOK 1 HR 30 MINS

8 cups vegetable stock

1 lb (450g) dry pinto beans, soaked

1 large white onion, halved

3 garlic cloves

1 tbsp vegetable oil

1 small Serrano chile, deseeded and minced

2 large tomatoes, chopped

12oz (354ml) dark Mexican beer

2 tbsp tomato paste

Salt and pepper

1 In a large stockpot, combine stock, pinto beans, 1 onion half, and 1 garlic clove. Bring to a boil then reduce to a simmer over medium heat and cook, covered, for 45 minutes to 1 hour until beans are tender, adding additional stock as needed.

2 Meanwhile, dice remaining 1 onion half and mince remaining 2 garlic cloves.

3 Remove the pot from heat, drain beans into a colander, and remove garlic clove and large onion pieces. Set beans aside and let dry.

4 Wipe out the pot. Add oil and return the pot to the stove over medium-low heat. Add diced onion half and cook for 2 to 3 minutes until soft. Add minced garlic and chile and cook for an additional minute.

5 Add pinto beans, tomatoes, beer, and tomato paste. Stir to combine. Simmer, covered, for 20 minutes, or until beer cooks off and liquid thickens slightly. Taste and season with salt and pepper. Serve immediately.

Pulse exchange
One pound dry **kidney beans** or **borlotti beans**, soaked, are a hearty substitute for pinto beans.

Nutrition per serving

Calories	270
Total Fat	2.5g
Saturated Fat	1.5g
Cholesterol	0mg
Sodium	430mg
Total Carbohydrate	45g
Dietary Fiber	11g
Sugars	6g
Protein	13g

BAKED DISHES & CASSEROLES

CURRIED BLACK GRAM STUFFED ONIONS

The nuttiness of black gram and quinoa mixed with creamy goat cheese makes these stuffed onions a unique vegetarian entrée.

MAKES 8 · PREP 30 MINS · COOK 1 HR

4 medium yellow onions

1 cup water

2 ¼ cups vegetable broth

½ tsp curry powder

½ tsp garam masala

1 cup dry tri-color quinoa

¾ cup cooked black gram

6oz (170g) crumbled goat cheese

¼ cup plus 2 tbsp chopped cilantro

Salt and pepper

1 Preheat the oven to 375°F (190°C). Trim both ends off onions and discard skin. Cut each onion horizontally in half to create 2 flat sections. To create a well for filling, with a spoon or melon baller gently scoop out middle of each onion half, leaving bottom of onion intact.

2 Arrange onions in an 8×8-inch (20×20cm) glass or ceramic baking dish, well-side up, and fill the bottom of the dish with water. Cover dish with foil and bake for 40 minutes, or until onions are tender.

3 Meanwhile, in a medium saucepan, combine broth, curry powder, and garam masala. Bring to a gentle boil and add dry quinoa. Return to a boil then reduce to a simmer and cook, covered, for 15 to 18 minutes until tender. Remove from heat and let sit, covered, for 5 minutes.

4 In a large mixing bowl, combine cooked and seasoned quinoa, black gram, goat cheese, and ¼ cup cilantro. Thoroughly combine. Taste and season with salt and pepper.

5 Spoon an equal amount quinoa mixture into each onion half. Bake, uncovered, for 20 minutes, or until filling is toasted and warmed through. Garnish with remaining 2 tablespoons cilantro and serve immediately.

● Make it with meat

Reduce cooked black gram to ½ cup and add ½ pound (225g) cooked ground lamb along with onion.

Nutrition per onion half

Calories	240
Total Fat	7g
Saturated Fat	3.5g
Cholesterol	10mg
Sodium	140mg
Total Carbohydrate	30g
Dietary Fiber	6g
Sugars	4g
Protein	12g

MOTH BEAN STUFFED SWEET POTATOES
WITH BRIE & POMEGRANATE

The surprising mix of sweet and savory in these baked potatoes makes for a truly luscious vegetarian meal or hearty side dish.

MAKES 8 · PREP 15 MINS · COOK 1 HR 15 MINS

4 medium sweet potatoes (about 2lbs; 1kg)

2 cups cooked moth beans

8oz (227g) Brie

Salt and pepper

1 cup pomegranate seeds

1 cup roughly chopped cilantro

1 Preheat the oven to 425°F (220°C) and line a baking sheet with aluminum foil.

2 Cut each potato in half lengthwise. Lightly spray each cut side with cooking spray. Arrange potatoes cut-side down on the baking sheet and bake for 30 to 40 minutes until fork tender all the way through.

3 To assemble, turn sweet potato halves cut-sides up. With a fork, fluff inside of sweet potatoes while keeping skin intact. Top each potato half with ¼ cup moth beans and 1 ounce (28g) Brie. Season with salt and pepper.

4 Bake for an additional 8 to 10 minutes until Brie is melted and gooey. Sprinkle each potato half with 2 tablespoons pomegranate seeds and 2 tablespoons chopped cilantro. Serve immediately.

Nutrition per sweet potato half

Calories	320
Total Fat	9g
Saturated Fat	5g
Cholesterol	30mg
Sodium	210mg
Total Carbohydrate	48g
Dietary Fiber	6g
Sugars	16g
Protein	15g

● **Make it with meat**

Crumble 2 ounces (55g) cooked bacon into each sweet potato along with pomegranate seeds.

ASIAN ADZUKI BAKED BEANS

The flavor profile of these baked beans is reminiscent of Korean BBQ—sweet and savory with gentle heat from the Gochujang.

SERVES 8 · PREP 20 MINS · COOK 1 HR 5 MINS

1 tbsp sesame oil

1 medium yellow onion, diced

1 tbsp tomato paste

½ cup firmly packed light brown sugar

2 ½ tbsp molasses

1 ½ tsp ground mustard

½ tsp ground ginger

2 tbsp Gochujang

1 tbsp rice wine vinegar

1 tbsp light soy sauce

6 cups cooked adzuki beans

¾ cup vegetable stock

Salt and pepper

1 Preheat the oven to 325°F (180°C). In a large skillet, heat sesame oil over medium-low heat. Add onion and cook for 2 to 3 minutes until soft. Add tomato paste, brown sugar, molasses, mustard, ground ginger, Gochujang, vinegar, and soy sauce. Cook for 2 to 3 minutes until mixture bubbles.

2 Add adzuki beans and stir to combine. Transfer bean mixture to a 2-quart (2l) glass baking dish. Pour in stock and stir gently to mix. Cover the dish with aluminum foil and cook for 30 minutes. Remove the foil and cook for an additional 20 minutes, or until it thickens. Serve immediately.

Nutrition per serving

Calories	320
Total Fat	2g
Saturated Fat	0g
Cholesterol	0mg
Sodium	220mg
Total Carbohydrate	62g
Dietary Fiber	13g
Sugars	20g
Protein	14g

●Make it with meat

For a smoky flavor, chop 2 slices raw bacon and cook with onions in step 1.

GREEK STUFFED TOMATOES

Dill and mint are tasty in stuffed tomatoes, served with the lids on for a fun presentation.

MAKES 6 · PREP 30 MINS · COOK 4 HR

6 large red tomatoes

¾ cup vegetable stock

3 tbsp olive oil

1 small yellow onion, finely diced

2 garlic cloves, minced

2 tbsp tomato paste

¼ cup chopped dill

¼ cup chopped mint

¼ cup chopped flat-leaf parsley

Zest and juice 1 lemon

1 cup cooked navy beans

1 cup cooked brown basmati rice

Salt and pepper

1 Preheat the oven to 400°F (200°C). Cut the top quarter off tomatoes and scoop out flesh. Place in a baking dish. Pour ½ cup stock into the dish.

2 In a large skillet, heat 1 tablespoon oil over medium-low heat. Add onion and cook for 2 to 3 minutes until soft. Add garlic and cook for 1 minute. Stir in tomato paste, dill, mint, parsley, lemon zest and juice, remaining ¼ cup stock, navy beans, and rice. Season with salt and pepper.

3 Portion filling equally into tomatoes and place tops on. Drizzle with remaining 2 tablespoons oil. Cover with foil and cook for 20 minutes. Remove foil and cook for an additional 20 minutes, or until tender. Serve immediately.

Nutrition per tomato

Calories	180
Total Fat	8g
Saturated Fat	1g
Cholesterol	0mg
Sodium	400mg
Total Carbohydrate	26g
Dietary Fiber	6g
Sugars	7g
Protein	5g

●Make it with meat

Cut navy beans to ½ cup and stir in 2 ½ ounces (70g) cooked ground lamb or beef into stuffing.

GREEN SPLIT PEA STUFFED CABBAGE

Cuisines from all over the world boast inspired versions of stuffed cabbage. This recipe uses green split peas for added texture in the filling.

MAKES 15 · PREP 50 MINS · COOK 1 HR 5 MINS

● **Make it with meat**

Leave out ½ cup cooked brown rice and add ½ pound (225g) cooked ground lamb or beef to rice mixture.

1 small head Savoy cabbage

2 tbsp olive oil

1 small yellow onion, diced

1 garlic clove, minced

¼ tsp red pepper flakes

1 bay leaf

2 thyme sprigs

28oz (794g) can crushed tomatoes

½ cup vegetable stock

1 tbsp balsamic vinegar

Salt and pepper

2 cups cooked brown rice

1 ½ cups cooked green split peas

½ cup chopped green olives

¼ cup toasted chopped walnuts

Zest and juice 1 lemon

Pinch cinnamon

1 Preheat the oven to 375°F (175°C). Bring a large pot of water to a boil. Cut core out of Savoy cabbage and select 15 leaves to stuff. With a paring knife, carefully remove hard stem of each leaf. Blanche leaves for 1 to 2 minutes until bright green and tender. Let dry on a kitchen towel.

2 In a medium saucepan, heat 1 ½ tablespoons oil over medium-low heat. Add onion and cook for 2 to 3 minutes until soft. Add garlic and cook for an additional minute. Stir in red pepper flakes, bay leaf, thyme, tomatoes, stock, and vinegar. Bring to a boil then reduce to a simmer and cook for 10 to 12 minutes. Taste and season with salt and pepper. Remove bay leaf and thyme stems.

3 Meanwhile, heat a large skillet over medium-low heat. Add remaining ½ tablespoon oil and warm until shimmering. Add brown rice, green split peas, olives, walnuts, lemon zest and juice, and cinnamon. Cook over low heat for 10 minutes, or until warmed through. Taste and season with salt and pepper.

4 Coat the bottom of a 9×13-inch (23×33cm) baking dish with some of tomato sauce mixture. Take one cabbage leaf and place on a clean, flat work surface. Place about 5 tablespoons rice filling on top of leaf and roll into a small bundle. Place seam-side down in the dish. Repeat with remaining leaves and filling. Cover stuffed cabbage evenly with remaining tomato sauce mixture.

5 Cover the dish with aluminum foil and bake for 20 minutes. Remove the foil and cook for another 15 to 20 minutes, basting periodically with sauce. Serve immediately.

Nutrition per cabbage leaf

Calories	120
Total Fat	4g
Saturated Fat	0g
Cholesterol	0mg
Sodium	140mg
Total Carbohydrate	20g
Dietary Fiber	6g
Sugars	5g
Protein	5g

LENTIL & QUINOA STUFFED POBLANOS

These large, mild peppers have a slightly smoky flavor when cooked and hold their shape well, making them excellent for this Tex-Mex stuffing.

MAKES 8 · PREP 20 MINS · COOK 30 MINS

4 poblano peppers
1 tbsp olive oil
1 cup cooked red quinoa
1 cup cooked beluga lentils
1 cup fresh corn kernels
1 tbsp ground cumin
1 ½ tsp chipotle chili powder
¼ tsp chili powder
½ tsp tomato paste
⅓ cup vegetable broth
½ cup chopped cilantro
8oz (225g) soft goat cheese

1 Preheat the oven to 375°F (190°C). Cut peppers in half lengthwise, leaving stems intact to create two full halves, and remove seeds. Drizzle with oil and arrange cut-side down in a 9×13-inch (23×33cm) glass baking dish. Roast for 10 minutes, or until tender but still maintaining shape.

2 Meanwhile, to make stuffing, in a large mixing bowl combine quinoa, lentils, corn, cumin, chipotle chili powder, chili powder, tomato paste, broth, cilantro, and 4 ounces (110g) goat cheese.

3 To assemble, fill each roasted pepper half with an equal amount quinoa mixture. Top each with ½ ounce (14g) remaining goat cheese. Return to the oven and bake for 15 minutes until warmed through. Serve immediately.

Nutrition per poblano half

Calories	290
Total Fat	11g
Saturated Fat	4.5g
Cholesterol	15mg
Sodium	150mg
Total Carbohydrate	38g
Dietary Fiber	7g
Sugars	1g
Protein	14g

Pulse exchange
Substitute an equal amount **pinto beans** or **black beans** instead of beluga lentils.

CHICKPEA FLOUR SOCCA
WITH HERB & GREEN OLIVE SALAD

Socca—a chickpea flour pancake—hails from the South of France. Its mild, nutty flavor is the perfect canvas for the fresh herbs and flavors of the arugula salad.

MAKES 2 · PREP 5 MINS, PLUS 1 HR FOR BATTER TO REST · COOK 15 MINS

1 cup chickpea flour

1 tsp smoked paprika

Dash garlic powder

Pinch salt

3 tbsp olive oil

1 cup water

2 cups arugula

½ cup flat-leaf parsley

¼ cup basil leaves

⅓ cup pitted green olives, halved

Juice 1 lemon

1 To make batter, in a medium mixing bowl, add chickpea flour, paprika, garlic powder, salt, 2 tablespoons oil, and water. Whisk to combine. Let rest at room temperature for 1 hour.

2 With the rack in the middle of the oven, place two 8-inch (20cm) cast-iron or ovenproof skillets in the oven and preheat to 450°F (232°C). (The skillets should heat up with the oven.)

3 When the skillets are heated, carefully remove and swirl 1 ½ teaspoons oil around in each skillet. Pour half of batter into each and return to the oven. Bake for 8 minutes. Then turn the broiler on low and cook for an additional 2 minutes. Remove from the oven and let rest for 1 to 2 minutes.

4 Meanwhile, to make herb and olive salad, toss together arugula, parsley, basil, olives, and lemon juice. Place each socca on a serving plate and top with equal amounts salad. Serve immediately.

Nutrition per socca

Calories	403
Total Fat	26g
Saturated Fat	3.5g
Cholesterol	0mg
Sodium	237mg
Total Carbohydrate	32g
Dietary Fiber	7g
Sugars	6g
Protein	12g

● **Make it with meat**

For a more filling meal, top salad with sliced, grilled steak.

RED LENTIL LASAGNA

This Italian comfort classic has all the rich creaminess of ricotta, mozzarella, and Parmesan with the added protein and fiber of red lentils.

● **Make it with meat**

Cook ½ pound (225g) ground turkey or beef along with onion in step 1 before adding garlic.

SERVES 12 · PREP 20 MINS · COOK 1 HR 30 MINS

1 tbsp olive oil

2 celery stalks, diced

2 small carrots, peeled and finely diced

1 medium yellow onion, diced

2 garlic cloves, minced

2 tsp chopped oregano

1 tsp chopped thyme

1 tsp chopped flat-leaf parsley

Pinch red pepper flakes

2 ½ cups dry red lentils

2 tbsp tomato paste

16oz (500g) tomato purée

16oz (500g) crushed tomatoes

½ cup vegetable stock

Salt and pepper

32oz (907g) ricotta cheese

1 large egg, beaten

2 ½ cups shredded Mozzarella cheese

2 tsp chopped basil

¼ cup grated Parmesan cheese

9oz (255g) box oven-ready lasagna sheets

1 Preheat the oven to 350°F (180°C). In a large Dutch oven, warm oil over medium-low heat. Add celery, carrots, and onion and cook for 2 to 3 minutes until soft. Add garlic and cook for an additional minute. Stir in oregano, thyme, parsley, and red pepper flakes.

2 Add lentils, tomato paste, tomato purée, crushed tomatoes, and stock. Bring to a boil then reduce to a simmer and cook for 20 to 25 minutes until lentils are tender. Taste and season with salt and pepper.

3 Meanwhile, in a large mixing bowl, stir together ricotta, egg, 1 cup Mozzarella, basil, and Parmesan.

4 To assemble, in a 9×13-inch (23×33cm) baking dish, lightly spread lentil mixture to coat the bottom of the dish. Layer with 3 lasagna sheets, a third ricotta mixture, then a third lentil mixture. Repeat layers two more times for 3 layers total. Finally, top with 3 lasagna sheets, dot top with any remaining lentil mixture, and sprinkle remaining 1 ½ cups Mozzarella cheese over top.

5 Cover the dish with aluminum foil and bake for 40 minutes. Remove the foil and cook for an additional 20 minutes. Let stand 5 to 10 minutes before serving.

Nutrition per serving

Calories	290
Total Fat	14g
Saturated Fat	8g
Cholesterol	55mg
Sodium	250mg
Total Carbohydrate	27g
Dietary Fiber	5g
Sugars	6g
Protein	17g

Why not try ...

Sauté 4 cups baby spinach and layer on top of ricotta throughout assembly.

BAKED FETA
IN TOMATO LENTIL SAUCE

A crowd-pleasing appetizer, this dish is easy and cozy. The hot, gooey feta and tangy, sweet tomato sauce will melt in your mouth, so scoop up every last drop with the baguette slices.

SERVES 4 · PREP 15 MINS · COOK 50 MINS

1 tbsp olive oil

1 garlic clove, minced

28oz (830ml) can crushed tomatoes

2 tsp chopped oregano

1 tbsp balsamic vinegar

Pinch red pepper flakes

½ cup cooked yellow lentils

Salt and pepper

8oz (226g) feta cheese block

1 baguette, cut into 1-in (2.5cm) slices, toasted

1 Heat the oven to 350°F (180°C). In a large saucepan, heat oil over medium-low heat until shimmering. Add garlic and cook for 2 to 3 minutes until soft but not browned.

2 Incorporate crushed tomatoes, oregano, vinegar, and red pepper flakes. Bring to a boil and add lentils. Simmer, covered, over medium-low heat for 15 minutes, or until tomato sauce is warmed through. Taste and season with salt and pepper.

3 Transfer tomato sauce to a 3-quart (3l) casserole or baking dish. Slice feta into ½-inch (1cm) rounds and arrange in an even layer on top of sauce.

4 Bake, uncovered, for 12 minutes, or until feta is soft and slightly melted. Serve immediately with baguette slices.

Nutrition per serving

Calories	330
Total Fat	16g
Saturated Fat	9g
Cholesterol	50mg
Sodium	950mg
Total Carbohydrate	34g
Dietary Fiber	8g
Sugars	12g
Protein	15g

Pulse exchange

Substitute an equal amount **red lentils** instead of yellow lentils.

BAKED LENTIL SPAGHETTI SQUASH
WITH WALNUTS & GOAT CHEESE

To infuse your diet with complex carbohydrates, spaghetti squash is a healthy alternative to pasta. Each squash half is its own nutty, casserole-type dish in a self-contained serving.

SERVES 2 · PREP 25 MINS · COOK 45 MINS

1 spaghetti squash

2 tbsp olive oil

1 ½ cups cooked green or Le Puy lentils

½ cup walnuts, toasted and roughly chopped

1 tbsp thyme leaves

Zest 1 lemon

Salt and pepper

4oz (110g) soft goat cheese

1 Preheat the oven to 375°F (190°C). Cut spaghetti squash in half lengthwise and use a spoon to scrape out seeds from each half. Drizzle each half with 1 tablespoon oil, and arrange cut-side down on a baking sheet. Cook for 30 to 35 minutes until tender but not mushy.

2 Meanwhile, in a medium mixing bowl, combine lentils, walnuts, thyme, and lemon zest. Set aside until squash is done.

3 With a fork, scrape squash flesh to expose and fluff spaghetti shreds. Season with salt and pepper to taste. Portion lentil filling evenly into each half and crumble goat cheese over each. Bake for an additional 10 minutes, or until cheese softens. Serve immediately, directly from squash shell.

Nutrition per serving

Calories	700
Total Fat	46g
Saturated Fat	12g
Cholesterol	25mg
Sodium	610mg
Total Carbohydrate	51g
Dietary Fiber	17g
Sugars	11g
Protein	30g

Pulse exchange

Use an equal amount **mung beans** in place of green or Le Puy lentils.

THREE BEAN PAELLA

This colorful twist on the classic Spanish dish features a trio of meaty pulses in addition to saffron-scented rice, roasted red peppers, and briny green olives.

SERVES 10 · PREP 35 MINS · COOK 1 HR 5 MINS

2 tbsp olive oil

1 medium yellow onion, chopped

3 garlic cloves, minced

Pinch saffron threads

Pinch red pepper flakes

1 cup crushed tomatoes

1 tsp smoked paprika

2 ½ cups dry Bomba or Calisparra rice

3 cups vegetable stock

¾ cup cooked navy beans

¾ cup cooked pigeon peas

¾ cup cooked kidney beans

½ cup frozen green peas, thawed

Salt and pepper

½ cup roasted red pepper strips

½ cup sliced green Spanish olives

1 large lemon, cut into 8 wedges

Flat-leaf parsley, to garnish

1 In a 10-inch (25cm) paella pan or large cast-iron skillet, warm oil over medium heat until shimmering. Add onion and cook for 2 minutes, or until it starts to soften. Stir in garlic and cook for 30 seconds, or until fragrant. Incorporate saffron, red pepper flakes, tomatoes, and paprika. Stir in rice and cook for 2 to 3 minutes.

2 Add stock to rice mixture and stir. Bring to a boil then reduce heat to low and cook, covered, for 20 minutes. Stir in navy beans, pigeon peas, and kidney beans. Cover again and cook for an additional 10 minutes. Scatter green peas across top and cook without stirring, covered, for an additional 10 minutes, or until beans and peas are warmed through. Remove from heat.

3 Taste and season with salt and pepper. Arrange roasted red pepper strips and olives evenly across top. Cover and let paella stand for 5 minutes. Garnish with lemon wedges and parsley, then serve.

Nutrition per serving

Calories	290
Total Fat	4.5g
Saturated Fat	0.5g
Cholesterol	0mg
Sodium	260mg
Total Carbohydrate	55g
Dietary Fiber	6g
Sugars	4g
Protein	8g

● **Make it with meat**

Add ½ pound (225g) cooked, peeled, and deveined shrimp along with red pepper strips in step 3.

LIMA BEAN ENCHILADAS

Tomatillos are a staple in Mexican sauces. Their tart, fruity flavor shines in this herbaceous enchilada sauce, wonderfully set off by buttery lima beans and a sweet medley of vegetables.

MAKES 10 · PREP 55 MINS · COOK 1 HR

1 ½ lbs (680g) tomatillos, husks removed, roughly chopped

2 medium jalapeños, deseeded and chopped

1 medium white onion, chopped

1 cup cilantro sprigs

⅔ cup vegetable broth

Salt and pepper

1 tbsp vegetable oil

1 garlic clove, minced

2 medium zucchini, diced

1 cup fresh yellow or white corn kernels

4 cups packed baby spinach

1 ½ tsp ground cumin

1 tsp ground coriander

Pinch red pepper flakes

1 ½ cups cooked lima beans

10 small white corn tortillas

8oz (266g) shredded Monterey Jack or Mozzarella cheese

½ cup chopped cilantro

1 Preheat the oven to 350°F (180°C). On a rimmed baking sheet, lightly coated with cooking spray, arrange tomatillos, jalapeños, and onion. Roast for 20 to 25 minutes until tender. Let cool slightly. To make sauce, transfer roasted vegetables to a blender and combine with cilantro sprigs and broth. Blend until completely smooth. Season with salt and pepper.

2 To make filling, in a large skillet heat oil over medium-low heat. Add garlic and cook for 1 to 2 minutes until soft. Add zucchini and corn and cook, covered, for an additional 2 to 3 minutes until zucchini starts to become tender. Stir in spinach, cumin, coriander, and red pepper flakes. Cover and cook for an additional 3 to 4 minutes until spinach slightly wilts. Stir in lima beans. Taste and season with salt and pepper. Remove from heat and let cool slightly.

3 Spray a 9×13-inch (23×33cm) glass or ceramic baking dish with cooking spray. Lightly coat the bottom with sauce. To assemble, work one tortilla at a time on a clean, flat work surface. Portion 4 tablespoons filling into tortilla and top with 1 ½ to 2 tablespoons Monterey Jack. Roll tightly and place seam-side down in the dish. Repeat to make 10 enchiladas in total.

4 Top enchiladas with remaining sauce. Sprinkle remaining Monterey Jack over top. Cover with aluminum foil and bake for 15 minutes. Uncover and bake for an additional 10 minutes, or until Monterey Jack melts. Garnish with chopped cilantro and serve immediately.

Make it with meat

Reduce zucchini to one and add 4 ½ ounces (130g) cooked, shredded chicken or pork to filling.

Nutrition per enchilada

Calories	180
Total Fat	6g
Saturated Fat	3g
Cholesterol	10mg
Sodium	340mg
Total Carbohydrate	23g
Dietary Fiber	5g
Sugars	5g
Protein	10g

Why not try...
Use crumbled queso fresco instead of shredded cheese. Place 1 tablespoon inside each and sprinkle remaining cheese on top.

MEXICAN TAMALE SKILLET PIE

Tamales are a traditional Mexican dish of masa (cornmeal) filled with meat or vegetables. Here, the tamale is the cornbread topping for a skillet of beans and spices.

SERVES 10 · PREP 40 MINS · COOK 45 MINS

● **Make it with meat**

Brown ½ pound (225g) raw ground beef or turkey along with garlic.

1 tbsp olive oil

1 medium yellow onion, diced

1 garlic clove, minced

1 small jalapeño, deseeded and minced

1 medium red bell pepper, deseeded and diced

1 medium zucchini squash, diced

Kernels from 3 yellow corn cobs (about 1 ½ cups)

1 tsp chipotle chili powder

1 tbsp ground cumin

14oz (411g) can diced tomatoes

2 tbsp tomato paste

¾ cup vegetable broth

1 ½ cups cooked pinto beans

1 cup cooked kidney beans

¾ cup all-purpose flour

¾ cup yellow cornmeal

1 tsp salt

1 tsp granulated sugar

¾ tsp baking powder

¼ tsp baking soda

¾ cup whole milk

1 large egg

3 tbsp unsalted butter, melted

1 Preheat the oven to 425°F (220°C). In a 10-inch (25cm) cast-iron or ovenproof skillet, warm oil over medium heat. Add onion and cook for 2 to 3 minutes until soft. Add garlic and jalapeño and cook for an additional minute.

2 Add bell pepper, zucchini, and corn. Cook for 2 to 3 minutes. Incorporate chipotle chili powder and cumin. Pour in diced tomatoes, tomato paste, broth, pinto beans, and kidney beans. Mix thoroughly. Bring to a boil then reduce to a simmer over low heat and cook for 8 to 10 minutes. Remove from heat.

3 Meanwhile, in a large mixing bowl, whisk together flour, cornmeal, salt, sugar, baking powder, and baking soda.

4 In another small bowl, mix together milk and egg. To make cornbread batter, add milk-egg mixture to flour mixture. Then drizzle in melted butter and stir.

5 To assemble, spread cornbread batter across the top. Bake for 15 minutes, or until cornbread is completely baked and lightly golden brown. Serve immediately.

Nutrition per serving

Calories	280
Total Fat	8g
Saturated Fat	3g
Cholesterol	30mg
Sodium	170mg
Total Carbohydrate	45g
Dietary Fiber	6g
Sugars	5g
Protein	7g

Pulse exchange

Substitute 2 cups cooked **pigeon peas** instead of kidney beans.

PIGEON PEA SAMOSA BAKE

Filled with the unique aromas and flavors of Indian spiced potatoes and pigeon peas, this approachable casserole with a crunchy phyllo top is a nod to traditional samosa pastry.

SERVES 8 · PREP 30 MINS · COOK 45 MINS

4 cups peeled and cubed Yukon Gold potatoes

1 cup frozen green peas, thawed

3 tbsp ghee

1 small yellow onion, diced

1 small green chile, deseeded and minced

¼ tsp ground ginger

¼ tsp ground coriander

¾ tsp garam masala

1 tsp ground cumin

¼ tsp turmeric

¼ tsp ground cayenne pepper

¾ tsp curry powder

1 tbsp water

½ cup cooked pigeon peas

⅓ cup vegetable stock

⅓ cup chopped cilantro

Salt and pepper

4 sheets frozen phyllo dough, thawed

Nutrition per serving

Calories	150
Total Fat	4.5g
Saturated Fat	2.5g
Cholesterol	5mg
Sodium	75mg
Total Carbohydrate	25g
Dietary Fiber	3g
Sugars	2g
Protein	4g

1 Preheat the oven to 350°F (180°C). Coat a 9-inch (23cm) round baking dish with cooking spray.

2 Bring a large pot of water to a rolling boil. Add potatoes and cook for 8 to 10 minutes until fork tender. Meanwhile, place green peas in a fine mesh sieve or colander. When potatoes are cooked through, pour potatoes and hot water over peas. Let drain thoroughly.

3 In a 12-inch (31cm) skillet, heat 2 tablespoons ghee over medium-low heat until shimmering. Add onion and chile and cook for 2 to 3 minutes until soft. Incorporate ginger, coriander, garam masala, cumin, turmeric, cayenne, curry powder, and water. Cook for an additional minute until spices are warmed through.

4 Add potatoes and green peas, pigeon peas, stock, cilantro, and remaining 1 tablespoon ghee. Stir to combine. Taste and season with salt and pepper. Remove from heat.

5 Transfer potato–pigeon pea mixture to the baking dish. Crinkle phyllo dough and place atop potato mixture. Bake for 20 to 25 minutes until phyllo dough is golden brown, then serve.

● **Make it vegan**

Replace ghee with vegetable or canola oil.

● **Make it with meat**

Add 4 ½ ounces (130g) cooked, seasoned ground lamb with peas in step 4.

Why not try...
For an aromatic garnish, sprinkle pastry with crushed cumin seeds before baking.

BLACK-EYED PEA CHILAQUILES

This traditional Mexican dish is an excellent way to use leftover tortillas. Baked with black-eyed peas and a savory, spicy tomato sauce, they are transformed into breakfast comfort food.

SERVES 4 · PREP 20 MINS · COOK 45 MINS

- 8 small white corn tortillas, cut into sixths
- 3 tbsp vegetable oil
- 2 garlic cloves, minced
- 1 ½ tsp dried oregano leaves
- 3 tsp ancho chili powder
- 1 ½ tsp ground cumin
- ½ tsp ground cayenne pepper
- 15oz (227g) can tomato sauce
- 1 cup water
- 1 cup cooked black-eyed peas
- 6oz (170g) crumbled queso fresco or Cotija cheese
- 3 green onions, white and green parts chopped
- 1 small jalapeño, thinly sliced
- 1 cup cilantro leaves

1 Preheat the oven to 325°F (170°C). To make tortilla chips, toss cut tortilla pieces in 2 tablespoons oil. Arrange on a baking sheet and bake for 15 to 20 minutes until crisp and golden brown.

2 Meanwhile, to make sauce, in a saucepan, heat remaining 1 tablespoon oil over medium-low heat. Add garlic and cook for 1 to 2 minutes until soft but not brown. Incorporate oregano, ancho chili powder, cumin, cayenne, tomato sauce, and water. Bring to a boil then reduce heat and simmer for 15 minutes, or until slightly thickened.

3 In a large mixing bowl, toss tortilla chips with black-eyed peas and about two-thirds of sauce. Arrange in a baking dish. Sprinkle queso fresco on top. Bake for 8 to 10 minutes until cheese is melted.

4 Garnish with green onion, jalapeño, and cilantro. Serve immediately with remaining sauce on the side.

● **Make it with meat**

Layer 4 ½ ounces (130g) cooked, shredded chicken or pork before adding cheese in step 3.

Nutrition per serving

Calories	380
Total Fat	18g
Saturated Fat	11g
Cholesterol	45mg
Sodium	750mg
Total Carbohydrate	41g
Dietary Fiber	7g
Sugars	6g
Protein	15g

Why not try...

Top with one runny, over-easy egg per portion and eat it for brunch.

GREEK EGGPLANT & LENTIL BAKE

This three-cheese casserole, inspired by Greek *moussaka*, combines lentils and eggplant for a rich and robust entrée.

SERVES 8 · PREP 45 MINS · COOK 1 HR 15 MINS

1 ½lb (225g) eggplant

3–4 tbsp olive oil

1 small yellow onion, finely diced

1 orange or yellow bell pepper, deseeded and diced

1 garlic clove, minced

2 tbsp tomato paste

1 ¼ cups cooked green or Le Puy lentils

1 ½ cups tomato purée

¼ tsp ground nutmeg

1 tsp cinnamon

Salt and pepper

1 cup Ricotta cheese

1 cup plain Greek yogurt

2oz (55g) crumbled Feta cheese

1 large egg

3 tbsp finely grated Parmesan cheese

2 tbsp chopped flat-leaf parsley, to garnish

1 Preheat the oven to 375°F (180°C). Coat a 2 ½ quart (2.5l) baking dish with cooking spray. Slice eggplant into ½-inch (1cm) thick rounds.

2 In a large nonstick skillet, heat ½ tablespoon oil over medium heat until shimmering. Working in batches, cook eggplant slices for 2 to 3 minutes per side until tender and lightly golden brown, adding an additional ½ tablespoon oil to the skillet between each flip. Remove slices from the skillet and place on a plate lined with a paper towel to absorb oil.

3 In the same skillet, heat remaining 1 tablespoon oil over medium-low heat until warm. Add onion and bell pepper and cook for 2 to 3 minutes until soft. Add garlic and cook for an additional minute.

4 Add tomato paste, lentils, tomato purée, nutmeg, and cinnamon. Stir to combine. Taste and season with salt and pepper and remove from heat.

5 Line the baking dish with a single layer of eggplant slices. Spread lentil mixture on top. Cover with another layer of remaining eggplant slices.

6 In a large mixing bowl, whisk together Ricotta, yogurt, Feta, and egg. Spread mixture evenly over eggplant. Sprinkle Parmesan over the top.

7 Bake for 30 to 35 minutes, uncovered, until top is set and golden brown. Garnish with parsley and let cool for 15 minutes before serving.

Nutrition per serving

Calories	240
Total Fat	13g
Saturated Fat	5g
Cholesterol	50mg
Sodium	430mg
Total Carbohydrate	19g
Dietary Fiber	6g
Sugars	7g
Protein	13g

SPICED SWEET POTATO SHEPHERD'S PIE

Sweet potato is a wonderful contrast to the warm spices in this Indian-inspired twist on a classic comfort dish.

SERVES 6 · PREP 35 MINS · COOK 50 MINS

3 medium sweet potatoes

⅓ cup heavy cream

Salt and pepper

2 tbsp ghee

1 medium yellow onion, chopped

1 garlic clove, minced

4 cups cooked brown lentils

1 tbsp ground cumin

1 tbsp garam masala

2 tsp curry powder

1 tsp turmeric

1 ⅔ cups vegetable stock

½ cup chopped cilantro

½ cup panko breadcrumbs

1 Preheat the oven to 375°F (190°C). Peel and cube sweet potatoes. In a large pot, bring 6 cups water to a boil. Cook potatoes for 15 to 20 minutes until fork tender. Drain thoroughly and transfer to a large mixing bowl. With a potato masher, mash potatoes and heavy cream until smooth. Season with salt and pepper to taste.

2 Meanwhile, in a large skillet, warm ghee over medium heat. Add onion and cook for 2 minutes, or until soft. Add garlic and cook for an additional minute.

3 Add lentils, cumin, garam masala, curry powder, and turmeric. Stir to combine and cook for 1 to 2 minutes to warm spices. Add stock and cook for 5 minutes. Stir in cilantro.

4 Pour lentil mixture evenly into a 3-inch (23×33cm) glass or ceramic baking dish. Top with mashed sweet potato. Bake for 15 minutes. Sprinkle evenly with breadcrumbs and bake for an additional 10 minutes, or until lightly browned. Cool for 10 minutes before serving.

Make it vegan

Substitute a vegan butter alternative or canola oil rather than ghee.

Make it with meat

Add 1 pound (450g) raw ground lamb. Reduce lentils by half and brown lamb along with onions.

Nutrition per serving

Calories	310
Total Fat	8g
Saturated Fat	4g
Cholesterol	20mg
Sodium	90mg
Total Carbohydrate	47g
Dietary Fiber	13g
Sugars	7g
Protein	14g

Pulse exchange

Instead of brown lentils, use an equal amount cooked **green lentils.**

KIDNEY BEAN CASSOULET

The flaky breadcrumb topping contrasts with the buttery kidney beans in this hearty and textured entrée.

SERVES 4 · PREP 20 MINS · COOK 1 HR

2 tbsp olive oil

1 small yellow onion, diced

1 carrot, diced

1 celery stalk, diced

2 garlic cloves, minced

3 thyme sprigs

1 bay leaf

Pinch red pepper flakes

3 ½ cups cooked kidney beans

¾ cup tomato purée

¾ cup vegetable stock

Salt and pepper

⅔ cup panko breadcrumbs

1 tbsp chopped flat-leaf parsley

1 Preheat the oven to 400°F (200°C). Lightly spray a 2-quart (2l) baking dish with cooking spray.

2 In a stockpot or Dutch oven, heat oil over medium-low heat. Add onion, carrot, and celery, and cook for 2 to 3 minutes until soft. Add garlic and cook for an additional minute.

3 Incorporate thyme, bay leaf, red pepper flakes, kidney beans, tomato purée, and stock. Simmer, covered, for 20 minutes.

4 Remove bay leaf and thyme stems. In a blender or food processor, purée ½ cup bean mixture until smooth. Return puréed mixture to the pot and stir to combine. Taste and season with salt and pepper. Transfer bean mixture to the baking dish.

5 To make topping, in a small bowl combine breadcrumbs and parsley. Top the dish evenly with breadcrumb mixture. Bake for 20 minutes, or until topping is golden brown. Serve immediately.

Nutrition per serving

Calories	330
Total Fat	8g
Saturated Fat	1g
Cholesterol	0mg
Sodium	95mg
Total Carbohydrate	51g
Dietary Fiber	14g
Sugars	5g
Protein	16g

● **Make it with meat**

Incorporate 4 ½ ounces (130g) cooked, shredded pork or duck just before transferring to the baking dish in step 4.

BROWN LENTIL & MUSHROOM POT PIE

Lentils and mushrooms covered in flaky puff pastry make a cozy, comforting meal.

SERVES 4 · PREP 25 MINS · COOK 45 MINS

1 tbsp olive oil

1 celery stalk, diced

1 small yellow onion, diced

2 carrots, diced

1 garlic clove, minced

1 tsp chopped rosemary

3 thyme sprigs

8oz (277g) cremini mushrooms, quartered

1 cup vegetable stock

2 tbsp tomato paste

2 tsp soy sauce

2 tsp cornstarch

2 tsp cold water

2 cups cooked brown lentils

Salt and pepper

1 sheet puff pastry (½ of 17.3oz; 440g pkg puff pastry)

1 Preheat the oven to 400°F (200°C). Coat a 1-quart (1l) baking dish with cooking spray. In a large skillet, heat oil over medium-low heat. Add celery, onion, and carrot. Cook for 2 to 3 minutes until soft. Add garlic and cook for 1 to 2 minutes.

2 Increase heat to medium and add rosemary, thyme, and mushrooms. Cook for an additional 4 to 5 minutes until mushrooms reduce in size and caramelize. Pour in stock, tomato paste, and soy sauce. Bring to a boil then reduce heat and simmer, covered, for 5 to 10 minutes until heated through.

3 In a small bowl, whisk together cornstarch and water. Add to mushroom mixture. Bring to a boil then reduce heat to low. Add lentils and stir to combine thoroughly. Cook, covered, for 5 minutes, or until liquid thickens. Taste and season with salt and pepper. Remove thyme stems.

4 Transfer lentil mixture to the baking dish. Cover with puff pastry sheet, rolling first if necessary to make fit. Trim sides so there is a 1-inch (3cm) overhang around the edges. Bake for 25 minutes, or until pastry is cooked and golden brown. Let sit for 5 minutes before serving.

Make it vegan

Replace soy sauce with an equal amount liquid aminos.

Make it with meat

To add umami flavor, use an equal amount beef stock rather than vegetable stock—taste before adding any additional salt.

Pulse exchange

Rather than brown lentils, use 2 cups cooked **green** or **Le Puy lentils**.

Nutrition per serving

Calories	440
Total Fat	20g
Saturated Fat	4g
Cholesterol	0mg
Sodium	350mg
Total Carbohydrate	50g
Dietary Fiber	11g
Sugars	7g
Protein	15g

SWEET POTATO & ADZUKI BEAN GRATIN

A golden breadcrumb crust tops this hearty gratin, flavored with savory sage and onion. Serve with bread and salad for a perfect autumn meal.

SERVES 6 · PREP 30 MINS · COOK 40 MINS

2 tbsp vegetable oil

1 large sweet potato, peeled and cubed

1 small yellow onion, diced

1 carrot, diced

1 garlic clove, minced

Pinch red pepper flakes

¾ tsp chopped sage

1 tsp soy sauce

1 cup vegetable stock

1 ½ cups cooked adzuki beans

¾ cup panko breadcrumbs

2 tbsp grated Parmesan cheese

Flat-leaf parsley, to garnish

1 Preheat the oven to 375°F (190°C). Toss 1 tablespoon oil with sweet potatoes. Arrange on a rimmed baking sheet and roast for 20 minutes, or until lightly caramelized and tender. Let cool slightly. Keep the oven heated.

2 In a large skillet, heat remaining 1 tablespoon oil over medium-low heat. Add onion and carrot and cook for 2 to 3 minutes until soft. Add garlic and cook for 1 to 2 minutes.

3 Stir in red pepper flakes, sage, soy sauce, stock, and adzuki beans. Add sweet potato. Cook over medium-low heat for 5 minutes, or until ingredients are heated through and liquid reduces.

4 In a small bowl, to make topping, combine breadcrumbs and Parmesan. Set aside.

5 Transfer sweet potato mixture to a 1-quart (1l) glass baking dish. Evenly top with breadcrumb mixture. Bake, uncovered, for 20 to 25 minutes until crispy and golden brown. Let sit for 5 minutes, then garnish with parsley and serve.

Make it vegan

Substitute nutritional yeast rather than Parmesan in topping.

Make it with meat

For added savory, smoky flavor, cook 1 ounce (25g) bacon along with onion.

Nutrition per serving

Calories	180
Total Fat	5g
Saturated Fat	4g
Cholesterol	0mg
Sodium	140mg
Total Carbohydrate	27g
Dietary Fiber	6g
Sugars	4g
Protein	6g

Why not try... For a fried sage garnish, in a shallow skillet, heat 1 tablespoon olive oil and fry 4 to 5 whole sage leaves for 10 to 15 seconds each.

DESSERTS

FLOURLESS BLACK BEAN BROWNIES

These brownies are not like any flourless baked good you've tried—they're light, moist, and cakey.

MAKES 12 · PREP 15 MINS · COOK 1 HR

2 cups cooked black beans
½ cup agave nectar
¼ cup coconut oil
1 tsp vanilla extract
Zest 1 medium orange
¼ tsp salt
½ tsp baking powder
⅓ cup granulated sugar
½ cup unsweetened cocoa powder
3 large eggs, beaten
½ cup semi-sweet chocolate chips

1 Preheat the oven to 350°F (180°C). Lightly spray an 11x7-inch (28x18cm) metal baking pan with cooking spray. In a food processor, combine black beans, agave, coconut oil, vanilla, and orange zest until smooth.

2 In a large mixing bowl, combine salt, baking powder, sugar, and cocoa powder. Incorporate black bean mixture and eggs.

3 Gently fold in chocolate chips, being careful not to over-mix batter.

4 Pour batter into baking pan. Bake for 30 to 35 minutes until brownies pull away from the pan and a toothpick inserted into center comes out clean. Let cool for 15 to 20 minutes before cutting and serving.

Nutrition per brownie

Calories	170
Total Fat	10g
Saturated Fat	7g
Cholesterol	45mg
Sodium	65mg
Total Carbohydrate	18g
Dietary Fiber	5g
Sugars	7g
Protein	5g

● Make it vegan

Replace eggs with 1 cup unsweetened applesauce.

COCONUT WHITE BEAN TRES LECHES CAKE

Tres leches cake is a traditional Mexican dessert that is soaked in three kinds of milk. Here, coconut milk adds a flavorful twist to the classic recipe.

SERVES 16 · PREP 30 MINS · COOK 30 MINS, PLUS 2 HRS 15 MINS TO COOL & CHILL

½ tsp baking powder

½ cup whole-wheat pastry flour

½ cup white bean flour

Pinch salt

5 large eggs, whites and yolks separated

1 cup granulated sugar

⅓ cup unsweetened almond milk

1 tsp vanilla extract

12oz (354ml) can evaporated milk

14oz (397g) can sweetened condensed milk

5.6oz (165 ml) can coconut milk

1 ½ cups heavy whipping cream

1 cup unsweetened, shredded coconut flakes, toasted

1 Preheat the oven to 350°F (180°C). Coat a 9x13-inch (23x33cm) glass baking dish with cooking spray. In a large mixing bowl, combine baking powder, whole-wheat pastry flour, white bean flour, and salt.

2 In a large mixing bowl, with the whisk attachment of an electric mixer, beat egg yolks and ¾ cup sugar for 2 to 3 minutes until a very pale, light yellow. Stir in almond milk and vanilla. Add egg-sugar mixture to flour mixture and stir to incorporate.

3 Clean out egg mixing bowl and add egg whites and remaining ¼ cup sugar. Beat whites on medium speed for 4 to 5 minutes until stiff peaks form. Gently fold egg white mixture into flour-egg mixture.

4 Transfer batter to the baking dish, spreading evenly and bake for 35 to 40 minutes until a toothpick inserted into center comes out clean. Let cool for 30 minutes.

5 Meanwhile, in a small saucepan, combine evaporated milk, condensed milk, and coconut milk. Bring to a boil, stirring occasionally, then remove from heat and let cool completely.

6 With a fork or wooden skewer, generously poke holes through cake. Evenly pour milk mixture over cake (you may not need the entire amount; milk should fill the dish about halfway). Cover with aluminum foil and refrigerate for 45 minutes, letting cake absorb milk.

7 Once cake has rested, in a small bowl whip heavy whipping cream until soft peaks form. Spread whipped cream evenly over top of cake then sprinkle with toasted coconut. Refrigerate once more for 1 hour or overnight. Store tightly covered in the refrigerator for up to 2 days.

Nutrition per serving

Calories	360
Total Fat	19g
Saturated Fat	12g
Cholesterol	105mg
Sodium	140mg
Total Carbohydrate	41g
Dietary Fiber	2g
Sugars	34g
Protein	8g

COCONUT & BEAN ICE CREAM

Homemade red bean paste makes this less cloyingly sweet than a commercial ice cream.

SERVES 8 · PREP 25 MINS, PLUS 2 HRS TO FREEZE

2 cups cooked adzuki
  beans
⅔ cup firmly packed light
  brown sugar
½ cup granulated sugar
1 ½ cups heavy cream

1 ½ cups whole milk
Pinch salt
⅔ cup sweetened,
  shredded coconut,
  toasted

1 To make paste, in a food processor, combine adzuki beans and brown sugar. Pulse until smooth. Transfer to a large mixing bowl.

2 In the mixing bowl, whisk in granulated sugar, heavy cream, milk, and salt.

3 In the frozen bowl of an electric ice cream maker, add cream mixture and churn for 15 to 20 minutes until the texture of soft serve ice cream. Add toasted coconut and churn for an additional minute, or until completely combined.

4 Remove ice cream mixture from the frozen bowl and transfer to an airtight, freezer safe storage container. Freeze for 2 hours or overnight before serving.

Nutrition per serving

Calories	400
Total Fat	20g
Saturated Fat	13g
Cholesterol	65mg
Sodium	135mg
Total Carbohydrate	52g
Dietary Fiber	5g
Sugars	37g
Protein	7g

● **Make it vegan**

Replace heavy cream with coconut cream and whole milk with coconut milk beverage.

ADZUKI BEAN & CHERRY POPS

The tartness of cherries are a wonderful match for the creaminess of the coconut milk and adzuki beans in this frozen treat.

MAKES 10 · PREP 15 MINS, PLUS 6 HRS TO FREEZE

12oz (340g) pitted dark
  sweet frozen cherries
½ cup cooked adzuki
  beans

13.5oz (400 ml) can
  coconut milk
3 tsp granulated sugar

1 Slightly thaw then roughly chop ¼ cup cherries and set aside. In a blender, combine adzuki beans, coconut milk, sugar, and remaining cherries. Purée until completely smooth. Strain mixture through a fine mesh sieve to remove tough skins.

2 Place approximately ¼ teaspoon chopped cherries in the bottom of each pop mold to make 10 pops total. Pour an equal amount blended adzuki bean mixture into molds. Insert wooden pop sticks into each. Freeze for 6 hours to overnight.

Nutrition per pop

Calories	100
Total Fat	7g
Saturated Fat	6g
Cholesterol	0mg
Sodium	10mg
Total Carbohydrate	9g
Dietary Fiber	1g
Sugars	5g
Protein	2g

LENTIL BAKLAVA

There's nothing like baklava—a sticky, rich treat of flaky filo pastry, nuts, and honey. Brown lentils add nutritional value to this decadent dessert.

MAKES 24 · PREP 1 HR · COOK 1 HR

1 cup granulated sugar

⅓ cup honey

¾ cup water

3 thyme sprigs

Juice and peel 1 large orange

2 cups chopped pistachios

2 cups chopped walnuts

2 cups cooked brown lentils

1 ½ tsp cinnamon

¾ tsp ground cardamom

Pinch salt

1 ½ sticks (12 tbsp) unsalted butter, melted

16oz (454g) package phyllo dough, thawed

1 In a small saucepan, to make syrup, combine ¼ cup sugar, honey, and water. Bring to a low boil, stirring occasionally, until sugar dissolves. Add thyme and orange juice and peel. Cook over medium-low heat for 10 minutes until slightly thickened. Remove peel and thyme stems. Remove from heat and let cool.

2 Meanwhile, in a large bowl, combine pistachios, walnuts, lentils, cinnamon, cardamom, remaining ¾ cup sugar, and salt.

3 Preheat the oven to 350°F (175°C). Prepare a clean, flat workspace. Brush the bottom and sides of a 9x13-inch (23x33cm) metal baking pan with melted butter. Trim phyllo dough to fit the pan and cover with a lightly damp cloth to prevent drying as you work.

4 Place 8 phyllo sheets into the bottom of the pan, brushing every other layer with butter. Spread about ⅓ nut mixture on top of layer and distribute evenly. Repeat this process 2 more times to form 3 nut layers total.

5 Top pastry with 8 more sheets phyllo dough, and generously brush top layer with melted butter. Score through layers of pastry with a sharp knife, making 24 square or diamond shaped pieces—cut ¾ through while leaving bottom intact.

6 Bake for 40 to 45 minutes until golden-brown. Let cool for 5 minutes. Cut through scored pieces to the bottom of the pan. Spoon cooled syrup over the cuts. Let cool completely. Refrigerate, covered, for at least 3 hours to overnight before serving. Store up to 3 days in an airtight container in the refrigerator.

Nutrition per piece

Calories	260
Total Fat	16g
Saturated Fat	6g
Cholesterol	20mg
Sodium	125mg
Total Carbohydrate	26g
Dietary Fiber	3g
Sugars	13g
Protein	5g

ADZUKI BEAN CHOCOLATE PUDDING

A little goes a long way—this chocolate pudding is rich, decadent, and nutty with a smooth texture. The recipe is a perfect match for a bright raspberry garnish and whipped cream.

SERVES 6 · PREP 10 MINS, PLUS OVERNIGHT TO SET · COOK 20 MINS

3 tbsp cornstarch

2 tbsp plus ⅓ cup water

1 cup cooked adzuki beans

1 cup unsweetened almond milk

2 tsp vanilla bean paste

¼ cup agave nectar

½ cup unsweetened cocoa powder

6 raspberries, to garnish

1 In a small bowl, whisk together cornstarch and 2 tablespoons water. Set aside.

2 In a blender, purée adzuki beans with remaining ⅓ cup water and ½ cup almond milk until smooth.

3 In a small saucepan, whisk together remaining ½ cup almond milk, vanilla bean paste, agave, cocoa powder, and puréed adzuki beans until completely smooth.

4 Heat almond milk mixture over low heat for 8 to 10 minutes until mixture comes to a low simmer, stirring occasionally to keep smooth. Remove from heat and let sit at room temperature for 10 minutes.

5 Portion evenly among 6 serving cups, cover, and refrigerate overnight to set. Top each serving with a raspberry before serving.

Nutrition per serving

Calories	110
Total Fat	1.5g
Saturated Fat	0.5g
Cholesterol	0mg
Sodium	35mg
Total Carbohydrate	24g
Dietary Fiber	5g
Sugars	10g
Protein	4g

Pulse exchange

Instead of adzuki beans, substitute ¾ cup cooked **black beans.**

STRAWBERRY & GREEN LENTIL CRISP

In this recipe, natural sweetness of the strawberries pairs well with the caramelized topping. Crisps are a great way to use leftover fruit, so you can substitute any kind you have on hand.

SERVES 6 · PREP 30 MINS · COOK 1 HR 10 MINS

1 cup cooked green lentils

1 ½lbs (680g) strawberries, hulled and quartered

2 tbsp light brown sugar

3 tsp vanilla extract

1 tbsp cornstarch

¾ cup whole-wheat flour

¾ cup coarsely chopped almonds

⅓ cup rolled oats

⅓ cup granulated sugar

1 ½ tsp cinnamon

½ cup unsalted butter, melted

1 Preheat the oven to 350°F (180°C). Spread lentils in an even layer on a rimmed baking sheet. Toast for 20 minutes, or until dry and crispy.

2 In an 8x8-inch (20x20cm) glass baking dish, combine strawberries, brown sugar, vanilla, and cornstarch. Spread in an even layer.

3 To make crisp topping, in a separate large mixing bowl combine lentils, whole-wheat flour, almonds, oats, sugar, and cinnamon. Drizzle in melted butter and gently combine. Dollop topping across top of strawberry mixture.

4 Bake, uncovered, for 40 minutes, or until strawberry mixture bubbles and topping browns. Let cool for 15 to 20 minutes before serving.

Nutrition per serving

Calories	450
Total Fat	23g
Saturated Fat	10g
Cholesterol	40mg
Sodium	0mg
Total Carbohydrate	54g
Dietary Fiber	9g
Sugars	25g
Protein	9g

Pulse exchange

Use an equal amount cooked **moth beans** or **black gram** instead of green lentils.

WHITE BEAN CREPES
WITH APRICOT SAUCE

Crepes are an easy dessert that's sure to impress. The tartness of the apricot sauce brightens the nutty white bean crepes.

MAKES 12 · PREP 30 MINS · COOK 50 MINS

½lb (225g) fresh apricots, pitted and roughly chopped

2 tbsp plus 2 tsp honey

Juice 1 medium orange

½ tsp vanilla bean paste

½ tbsp orange marmalade

¼ cup water

1 cup white bean flour

2 ½ tbsp granulated sugar

1 tsp cinnamon

2 tbsp vegetable oil

½ cup water

1 cup unsweetened almond milk

2 tbsp vanilla extract

2 large eggs

Zest 1 large orange

½ cup chopped, toasted hazelnuts

Toasted coconut, to garnish

1 To make apricot sauce, in a medium saucepan combine apricots, honey, orange juice, vanilla bean paste, orange marmalade, and water. Bring to a boil then reduce heat and simmer, covered, for 20 minutes, stirring occasionally. Let cool then transfer to a blender and purée until smooth. Set aside.

2 To make crepe batter, in a large mixing bowl combine white bean flour, sugar, and cinnamon. In a separate medium mixing bowl, whisk together oil, water, almond milk, vanilla, eggs, and orange zest. Pour almond milk mixture into flour mixture and stir until completely combined and without lumps.

3 Heat a crepe pan or a 6-inch (15cm) nonstick skillet over medium heat. Pour in 4 tablespoons batter and gently swirl around the bottom of the pan. Cook for 1 to 2 minutes until set and pulling away from the sides. Gently flip and cook for an additional 1 to 2 minutes. Repeat to make 12 crepes total.

4 To serve, roll or fold crepes, drizzle with apricot sauce, and sprinkle toasted hazelnuts and coconut on top.

Nutrition per crepe

Calories	130
Total Fat	5g
Saturated Fat	2g
Cholesterol	30mg
Sodium	25mg
Total Carbohydrate	25g
Dietary Fiber	4g
Sugars	10g
Protein	4g

Why not try ...

Instead of hazelnuts, garnish with an equal amount toasted almonds.

CRANBERRY PISTACHIO BISCOTTI

Biscotti are Italian cookies that have a two-step baking process, wonderfully textured here with chewy cranberries and crunchy pistachios. Enjoy with coffee or tea for a lightly sweet treat.

MAKES 12 · PREP 25 MINS · COOK 1 HR 20 MINS

1 ¾ cups chickpea flour

1 tsp baking powder

¼ cup coconut oil, slightly warmed

¾ cup granulated sugar

2 tsp vanilla extract

2 large eggs

Zest 1 large orange

Pinch ground nutmeg

½ cup dried cranberries

¾ cup coarsely chopped pistachios

1 Preheat the oven to 300°F (150°C). Line a rimmed baking sheet with parchment paper. In a large mixing bowl, combine chickpea flour and baking powder.

2 In a medium mixing bowl, whisk together coconut oil, sugar, vanilla, eggs, orange zest, and nutmeg. To make batter, in the large mixing bowl, fold oil-sugar mixture into flour mixture until incorporated. Gently stir in cranberries and pistachios until just incorporated.

3 Transfer batter to the sheet and form into a flat, rectangular loaf, about 1-inch (3cm) tall. Bake for 35 minutes, or until lightly brown and set through the center. Let cool for 15 to 20 minutes.

4 Transfer the parchment paper to a flat work surface. Cut loaf into 12 equal strips. Transfer the parchment paper back to the baking sheet. Flip strips onto their cut sides, and evenly space on the sheet. Bake again for 20 minutes, or until firm and lightly golden brown. Let cool completely before serving, or store in an airtight container in the refrigerator for 2 to 3 days.

Nutrition per cookie

Calories	180
Total Fat	7g
Saturated Fat	4.5g
Cholesterol	30mg
Sodium	20mg
Total Carbohydrate	25g
Dietary Fiber	2g
Sugars	17g
Protein	4g

Why not try...

Use an equal amount almond extract and chopped almonds rather than vanilla and pistachios.

CHICKPEA & PEANUT COOKIES

These cookies have the nutritional boost of chickpeas, plus they're naturally gluten-free.

MAKES 20 · PREP 45 MINS · COOK 15 MINS

1 cup cooked chickpeas
½ cup creamy peanut butter
1 large egg, lightly beaten
1 tsp vanilla extract
½ cup granulated sugar
¾ tbsp agave nectar

1 Preheat the oven to 350°F (180°C). In a food processor, pulse chickpeas until the consistency of coarse almond meal. Transfer to a medium mixing bowl.

2 Incorporate peanut butter, egg, vanilla, sugar, and agave. Stir to combine. Refrigerate for 30 minutes.

3 Line a baking sheet with parchment paper. Portion out 1 tablespoon batter, roll into a ball, and place on sheet. Repeat to use all batter. With a spatula, flatten dough into rounds.

4 Bake cookies for 7 minutes, then rotate the sheet 180 degrees and bake for an additional 7 to 8 minutes until set and lightly golden brown. Let cool to room temperature before removing from baking sheet. Store in an airtight container for up to 2 days.

Nutrition per cookie

Calories	80
Total Fat	3.5g
Saturated Fat	1g
Cholesterol	10mg
Sodium	5mg
Total Carbohydrate	9g
Dietary Fiber	1g
Sugars	7g
Protein	3g

●Make it vegan

Substitute 1 ripe banana rather than egg in batter.

THREE CITRUS POLENTA CAKE

This not-too-sweet cake brightly blends the flavors of lemon, orange, and grapefruit.

SERVES 10 · PREP 30 MINS · COOK 45 MINS

¼ cup fluid coconut oil
3 large eggs
Zest and juice 1 lemon (about 4 ½ tsp juice)
Zest and juice 1 orange (about ⅓ cup juice)
Zest and juice 1 grapefruit (about ½ cup juice)
1 ¼ cups cornmeal
¾ cup chickpea flour
1 ¼ tsp baking powder
½ cup granulated sugar
¼ cup confectioners' sugar

1 Preheat the oven to 350°F (180°C). In a small mixing bowl, whisk together coconut oil, eggs, lemon zest and juice, orange zest and juice, and grapefruit zest and juice.

2 In another large mixing bowl, whisk together cornmeal, chickpea flour, baking powder, and sugar. Fold in fruit mixture until just combined.

3 Pour batter into a greased 8-inch (20cm) springform pan. Place the pan on a baking sheet and bake for 30 to 35 minutes until set and a toothpick inserted into center comes out clean. Let rest in the springform pan for 10 minutes before removing side of pan. Dust with confectioners' sugar and serve.

Nutrition per serving

Calories	210
Total Fat	8g
Saturated Fat	5g
Cholesterol	55mg
Sodium	30mg
Total Carbohydrate	32g
Dietary Fiber	2g
Sugars	16g
Protein	5g

●Make it vegan

Mix 3 tablespoons ground flax seed with 9 tablespoons water rather than eggs in batter.

BERRY & LIME MUNG BEAN POPS

Refreshingly tart and naturally sweet, these pops are the perfect low-calorie treat for a hot day.

MAKES 10 · PREP 20 MINS, PLUS 6 HRS TO FREEZE

1 ½ cups blueberries
2 cups blackberries
⅓ cup cooked mung beans
3 tbsp lime juice
⅓ cup agave nectar
⅓ cup water

1 In a blender or food processor, purée blueberries, blackberries, mung beans, lime juice, agave, and water until completely smooth.

2 Pour mixture through a fine mesh sieve to remove seeds. Press mixture against the sieve to retain as much liquid as possible.

3 Pour liquid into 10 pop molds. Insert wooden pop sticks into each mold. Freeze for at least 6 hours or overnight before serving.

Pulse exchange

Use ½ cup cooked **moth beans** instead of mung beans.

Nutrition per pop	
Calories	45
Total Fat	0g
Saturated Fat	0g
Cholesterol	0mg
Sodium	0mg
Total Carbohydrate	11g
Dietary Fiber	2g
Sugars	7g
Protein	1g

INDEX

Entries in **bold** indicate ingredients.

ACKNOWLEDGMENTS

ABOUT THE AUTHOR

Tami Hardeman is a professional food stylist for both print and video. Her work is found in countless magazines, cookbooks, and advertisements. She is also a recipe developer and the author behind the internationally recognized food blog *Running with Tweezers*. Tami's recipes and photos have been featured by *CNN*, *The Huffington Post*, *Saveur*, and many more.

THANKS

I would like to thank Alexandra Elliott and the entire team at DK Alpha for their confidence, patience, and guidance. I cannot express my gratitude and love enough to Helene Dujardin, Rachael Daylong, and Abby Gaskins for making these lovely photos come to life. Much appreciation to my family and friends for being my constant cheerleaders. Nothing would be possible— my life, my career, or this book—without the unwavering love, care, and support of my husband, Mike Boutté. I love you, Boop. This book is dedicated to Philis.

DK would like to thank the following:
Recipe tester: Carolyn Doyle
Proofreader: Laura Caddell
Indexer: Heather McNeill

Acquisitions editor: Ann Barton
Development editor: Alexandra Elliott
Book designers: Mandy Earey, Philippa Nash, and William Thomas
Art director: Nigel Wright
Photographer: Helene Dujardin
Food stylist: Tami Hardeman
Jacket designer: Nicola Powling
Associate publisher: Billy Fields
Publisher: Mike Sanders

First American Edition, 2017
Published in the United States by DK Publishing
6081 E. 82nd Street, Indianapolis, Indiana 46250

Published in the United States by
Dorling Kindersley Limited.

ISBN: 978-1-4654-5919-0

Library of Congress Catalog Number: 2016950732

Printed and bound in China

All images © Dorling Kindersley Limited
For further information see: www.dkimages.com

A WORLD OF IDEAS:
SEE ALL THERE IS TO KNOW
www.dk.com

Note:

This publication contains the opinions and ideas of its author(s). It is intended to provide helpful and informative material on the subject matter covered. It is sold with the understanding that the author(s) and publisher are not engaged in rendering professional services in the book. If the reader requires personal assistance or advice, a competent professional should be consulted. The author(s) and publisher specifically disclaim any responsibility for any liability, loss, or risk, personal or otherwise, which is incurred as a consequence, directly or indirectly, of the use and application of any of the contents of this book.

Trademarks:

All terms mentioned in this book that are known to be or are suspected of being trademarks or service marks have been appropriately capitalized. Alpha Books, DK, and Penguin Random House LLC cannot attest to the accuracy of this information. Use of a term in this book should not be regarded as affecting the validity of any trademark or service mark.

DK books are available at special discounts when purchased in bulk for sales promotions, premiums, fund-raising, or educational use. For details, contact: DK Publishing Special Markets, 345 Hudson Street, New York, New York 10014 or SpecialSales@dk.com.